PENGUIN BOOKS

AMERICANS

Eric Schlosser is the author of *Fast Food Nation* and
Reefer Madness. This is his first play.

Americans

ERIC SCHLOSSER

PENGUIN BOOKS

PENGUIN BOOKS

Published by the Penguin Group
Penguin Books Ltd, 80 Strand, London WC2R ORL, England
Penguin Putnam Inc., 375 Hudson Street, New York, New York 10014, USA
Penguin Books Australia Ltd, 250 Camberwell Road, Camberwell, Victoria 3124, Australia
Penguin Books Canada Ltd, 10 Alcorn Avenue, Toronto, Ontario, Canada M4V 3B2
Penguin Books India (P) Ltd, 11 Community Centre, Panchsheel Park, New Delhi – 110 017, India
Penguin Books (NZ) Ltd, Cnr Rosedale and Airborne Roads, Albany, Auckland, New Zealand
Penguin Books (South Africa) (Pty) Ltd, 24 Sturdee Avenue, Rosebank 2196, South Africa

Penguin Books Ltd, Registered Offices: 80 Strand, London WC2R ORL, England

www.penguin.com

First published 2003
1

Set in 10/13 pt PostScript Adobe Sabon
Typeset by Rowland Phototypesetting Ltd, Bury St Edmunds, Suffolk
Printed in England by Clays Ltd, St Ives plc

for my parents, and Bob and Lola

Contents

Act I

Scene One

[*The curtain rises but the stage remains dark.*]

VOICE: Ladies and gentlemen; fellow Americans and distinguished visitors from around the world . . . the President of the United States . . . William McKinley. [*Pause. Then the same voice but deeper.*] It is with great pride that I declare the Pan American Exposition of 1901 officially open . . .

[*A large electric sign lights up across the rear of the stage, with* PEACE TO PAN AMERICA *spelled out in pink light bulbs, and beneath that, a huge American flag waving in red, white and blue lights. The voice in the dark was that of* MILBURN, *who stands center-stage behind a podium draped in bunting. His sleeves are rolled up, and he holds a large lever in his right hand, with which he has just turned on the lights.* MARK HANNA, *big, fat, balding, and formally attired, stands stage left, hands on hips, staring at the sign.* JONAS, *a wiry old man in a work shirt and overalls, leans on a ladder near the sign. For a moment, the sign shines brightly. But then section by section it slowly flickers and goes out. The stage, however, remains lit.*]

HANNA: Uh-oh. There goes New York. There goes New Jersey, Michigan, Ohio. [*The flag goes out completely.*] That's not a good sign.

MILBURN: She was working perfectly yesterday.

HANNA: Nobody cares about yesterday.

MILBURN [*stepping down from the podium*]: Don't you worry, Mr. Hanna. Jonas here is the finest electrician in all of Buffalo.

HANNA: All of Buffalo?

MILBURN: In all of New York State. There's thousands of wires back there, and he's familiar with every one of them.

[JONAS *takes the ladder behind the sign and goes to work.*]

HANNA: Tell me, Jonas, what do you think of these new electrical washing machines? Have you got one? Which model do you think is the best?

[*Pause*]

MILBURN: He doesn't have one.

HANNA: Oh.

MILBURN: He don't have any electricity in his house.

HANNA: There's no electricity in your house?

JONAS [*from behind the sign*]: Nope.

HANNA: Why not?

JONAS: Just don't.

MILBURN: It's his wife. She won't let him. [*Enjoying this*] Tell Mr. Hanna, Jonas. Tell him why not.

[*Pause*]

HANNA: Is she afraid?

MILBURN: You might say. Tell Mr. Hanna.

JONAS [*peering from behind the sign*]: Why the fuss, Milburn?

HANNA: Is she afraid of a fire?

MILBURN: Go ahead.

JONAS [*matter of factly*]: Senator, my wife's afraid of everything. [*Pause*] She says the End is near, the big Apocalypse is coming. Right now, she says, there's Antichrists roaming the earth, deceiving the multitudes with all kinds of miracles, making fire come down from the heavens and imprisoning it for the sight of man – that sort of thing. She blames Tom Edison, thinks he's one of Satan's top boys. [*Pause*] She says we'll soon witness spirits of demons performing signs, nation rising against nation, the war of Gog and Magog, earthquakes, famines, plagues, rivers of blood, mountains become molten, valleys cleft as wax before a flame. She says it could be any day now. [*Pause*] And she says it a lot.

HANNA: Oh.

MILBURN: What a woman.

HANNA: Well, does she, uh . . . condemn you to eternal damnation, on account of your work?

JONAS: No, sir. Long as I don't bring any of it home with me.

MILBURN: Isn't that something? And she won't cook!

HANNA: Don't you ever miss the conveniences, all the amenities you install for other folks?

JONAS: Well I try not to spend too much time around the house.

[*Blackout*]

Scene Two

[*Lights up on the same scene. The sign works perfectly. WILLIAM MCKINLEY stands behind the podium. He's in his late fifties, tall and rotund, solemn and dignified, a man buttoned up early in life and never unbuttoned. He speaks slowly and deliberately, without flourish.*]

MCKINLEY: Expositions are the time-keepers of Progress. And this exposition, in particular, makes abundantly clear how prosperous and how peaceful the Twentieth Century promises to be. I welcome to Buffalo the many representatives from our sister republics in Latin America. Let us look forward to a future bright with even warmer sentiments, with even closer cooperation among all the nations of this hemisphere. [*Pause*] The miracle-work of man's technology will inevitably link us all together with unbreakable bonds. Already steam and electricity, the telegraph and now the telephone, have annihilated the space and time between peoples. Wonderful inventions, beyond our imagination, are bound to draw us even closer in years to come. [*Pause*] In such a world, the United States can no longer stand aloof, can no longer maintain a policy of Isolation. Our recent victory in the war with Spain has opened our eyes to the endless opportunities for doing good on behalf of mankind. We will obey our sacred duty to Civilization in all our new territories – in the Philippines, Hawaii, Puerto Rico – wherever destiny may raise the Stars and Stripes one day. [*Pause*] And all the world shall soon look to America and see the wonders this liberty-loving and Christian people can achieve.

[*Loud applause and cheering.* MCKINLEY *waves to the audience, enjoying the ovation. Then he steps down from the podium and is joined by a young* GUIDE. *The lights dim, save for a spotlight which follows the two as they tour the Exposition.*]

GUIDE: The Streets of Mexico is an exact reproduction of your typical town square south of the border.

MCKINLEY: They wear those hats, do they?

GUIDE: Yes they do.

MCKINLEY: Charming.

[*They wander elsewhere.*]

MCKINLEY: That would be ice?

GUIDE: Yes it would. Because of the heat, we've used ordinary bricks and painted them, well, not white, but opal. Is that it? Opalescent.

MCKINLEY: I think so.

GUIDE: Up north it's ice.

MCKINLEY: You poor fellow, take off that fur coat, we'll go look at something else.

[*They wander elsewhere.*]

GUIDE: Have you ever seen one that size before?

MCKINLEY [*laughing*]: Heavens, no!

GUIDE: I never have.

MCKINLEY: What a potato!

GUIDE: It was grown by Daniel Huggins of Preston, Idaho. [*They reach the foot of the stage on the left*] Here we are . . . the Temple of Music.

MCKINLEY: How beautiful.

GUIDE: A shrine dedicated to the divine power of music, which can lift man's soul joyously to the heavens.

[*An organ plays Bach's* Sonata in F.]

MCKINLEY: I don't recognize this.

GUIDE: Bach, I think.

MCKINLEY: Oh, of course.

GUIDE: The reception is about to begin.

[*The guide steps back, leaving* MCKINLEY *alone. The rest of the stage is dark.* MCKINLEY *greets visitors as they pass by in an imaginary receiving line.*]

MCKINLEY: Why hello there! [*Pause*] A glorious day, indeed. [*Pause*] No, I missed the Indian village. [*Pause*] Fairbanks? Fairbanks, Alaska? That is quite a ways.

[LEON CZOLGOSZ *appears at the foot of the stage, on the right, waiting in line. He looks like a farm boy dressed in his Sunday best, wearing a dark suit and a starched white shirt. He's in his late twenties, handsome, with long, light brown hair. He makes his way in the line, slowly approaching* MCKINLEY. *The only unusual thing about* CZOLGOSZ

5

is his left hand, which appears to have been injured. It is wrapped in a white handkerchief.]

MCKINLEY: No, she's resting today, but I'll make sure to tell her. [*Pause*] My pleasure. [*Pause*] Oh, I'll shake the hand of a Democrat. [*Pause*] Isn't she darling! Looks just like her mother. [*Pause*] It does make one think.

[CZOLGOSZ *finally reaches* MCKINLEY *and extends his right hand.* MCKINLEY *grasps it firmly and looks him straight in the eye.*]

MCKINLEY: My dear boy, does it hurt?

[*Keeping hold of* MCKINLEY *with his right hand,* CZOLGOSZ *raises his left one. Then* CZOLGOSZ *fires two loud shots with a revolver hidden in the handkerchief.* MCKINLEY *stumbles backward a few steps. Blood splatters everywhere. Blackout. The scene ends in the dark with the sounds of a large crowd in chaos.*]

VOICES: Get the gun, Al, get the gun . . . Oh my God . . . Out of the way, please . . . Out of the way, everyone, out of the way . . .

Scene Three

[*Lights up on* DR MATTHEW D. MANN, *who stands center-stage. He has an immaculate gray beard and a rather pompous look.*]

MANN: My name is Doctor Matthew D. Mann. That's M–A–N–N. [*Pause*] I was in front of the Aerio Cycle, shaking hands with Buffalo Bill, when I heard someone say that a doctor was urgently needed at the Exposition hospital. I had no idea, until I arrived there, that the President of the United States was to be my patient. [*Pause*] Dr. Roswell

Park, our local expert on gunshot wounds, was in Niagara Falls and I did not think we could afford to wait for his arrival. [*Pause*] Although my own specialty is gynecology and obstetrics, I felt fully qualified to perform this medical procedure. Assisted by Doctors Mynter, Lee and Parmenter, I went to work at once. [*Pause*] The first bullet struck the patient on the breastbone, but did not penetrate further. The slug has been recovered and the wound presents no risk. The second bullet entered the patient's abdomen five inches below the left nipple, but we could not find that bullet, despite a long and careful search. [*Pause*] We found no damage to any vital organs. The President stood the operation well, and his condition justifies every hope of recovery. [*Pause*] Should you gentlemen have any further questions, I will be taking my supper at the grill in the Union Hotel. But I would prefer, at this time, not to be photographed. Thank you.

[*Blackout*]

Scene Four

[*A room at the Buffalo police station.* CZOLGOSZ *sits on a wooden stool, surrounded by Police Superintendent* WILLIAM BULL, *Secret Service agent* FOSTER *and* WASH-BURN, *a guard.*]

BULL: What is your name?

[CZOLGOSZ *ignores him.*]

FOSTER: Your *name*.

BULL: My name is William Bull. What's yours? [*Leans over.*] I'm superintendent of the Buffalo police. This is Foster of the Secret Service and that's Washburn. May we have the pleasure?

7

[*Pause. Then* FOSTER *suddenly strikes* CZOLGOSZ *in the face, knocking him off the stool and on to his back.* WASHBURN *picks him up roughly, pulling his hair.* FOSTER *raises his fist again, but* BULL *intervenes.*]

BULL: Boys, boys, go easy. We just want to talk.

[CZOLGOSZ *settles back on to the stool, holding the left side of his face.*]

FOSTER: There's a crowd out there screaming for your neck.

BULL: Must be two or three thousand of them.

WASHBURN: I say hand him over.

FOSTER: About an hour ago we caught someone trying to burn this building down.

WASHBURN: Hand him over to the people, they'll know what to do.

BULL: Who are you? Why did you do this?

FOSTER: Why?

BULL: Did someone pay you to? Was anyone with you?

FOSTER: You better talk.

BULL: Are you an anarchist? A socialist?

FOSTER: Union scum?

BULL: Who are you? Why did you do this?

WASHBURN: What's your name?

FOSTER: Are you some lunatic?

WASHBURN: Maybe he don't speak English. [*Loudly*] Who the hell are you?

FOSTER: *Sprecken ze Deutche?*

WASHBURN: You goddamn better talk.

BULL: Why did you do this? [*Pause*] Why did you shoot the President?

[FOSTER *punches* CZOLGOSZ *in the face, knocking him off the stool again with a loud crash. Blackout.*]

Scene Five

[IDA MCKINLEY *sits in a rocking chair, knitting a blue playsuit for an infant. Though attractive, she looks quite frail and her movements are odd and quirky. Beside her sits* DORIS, *a younger companion. In the background, there is the sound of a grandfather clock ticking.* IDA *hums to herself for a few moments, as she knits, then suddenly stops.*]

IDA: Does your husband smoke? Did I ask you that?

DORIS: Yes, you did.

IDA: Well, does he?

DORIS: Yes.

IDA: Could you open a window, please? There's a little bit of smoke left in this room. [DORIS *goes to the window.*] Thank you, dear. Dr. Rixey says even a little bit of smoke is a little bit too much for me.

DORIS: John promised me he hadn't smoked in here all week. I am so sorry.

IDA: It's not your fault. I just can't bear the slightest bit of smoke. [*Pause*] The President smokes twenty Garcias a day, can you imagine?

DORIS: Twenty?

IDA: And not one of them near me. Never in the same room, never in the room I'm about to enter.

DORIS: Oh, how dear.

IDA: And never in the carriage. Never. He has all day to smoke them, he doesn't need to smoke them near me.

DORIS: I wish John could hear this.

IDA: He knows I don't mind the smell, and I don't mind it, it's a manly smell. It's the smoke. I can't bear the slightest bit of smoke, and he knows that.

[IDA *returns to her knitting. An awkward silence.*]

DORIS: What did you think of Niagara Falls?

IDA: Do you have the time, dear?

DORIS: Yes, it's six o'clock. They seem to be running late.

IDA: The President loves to shake hands.

[*Long pause*]

DORIS: Did you enjoy your trip to Niagara Falls?

IDA: It was quite a strain.

DORIS: Everyone was so glad to see you make an appearance.

IDA: These things are quite a strain for me.

DORIS: You looked wonderful.

IDA: I'm always so afraid in front of the photographers.

DORIS: Everyone loved seeing you there.

IDA: It was such a relief to get back to the house.

DORIS: What did you think of the Falls?

IDA: Doris, dear, could you close the window, please? I think now there's a slight draft. I feel a chill.

DORIS: Of course.

[DORIS *returns to the window.* IDA *continues to knit. Awkward silence.*]

IDA: Did I ask what your husband does?

DORIS: Perhaps you didn't. John's a lawyer here in Buffalo.

IDA: A lawyer? I see. Any interest in politics?

DORIS: As a matter of fact . . .

[HANNA *arrives, and the two women look up at him, slightly surprised to see him alone.*]

HANNA: Ida.

[*Pause*]

IDA: Oh Lord, he's been shot.

[*Blackout*]

Scene Six

[CZOLGOSZ *is still sitting on the stool, but looks like a mess: his clothes are bloody from the shooting and his face is now battered and bruised.* WASHBURN *stands behind him, while* FOSTER *paces the cell. After a moment,* BULL *enters, along with* JOHN NOWAK, *a short, fat slob.*]

BULL: We took your picture on a tour of local flophouses, and look what we found.

NOWAK: That's him!

FOSTER: Who's this guy?

NOWAK: That's him, all right!

BULL: Mr. Nowak rents a few rooms above his saloon on the east side.

NOWAK: You little insect. I hope they hang you.

BULL: Did you rent a room from Mr. Nowak?

[CZOLGOSZ *ignores him.*]

NOWAK: Yes, you did.

WASHBURN: He hasn't said a word since you left.

NOWAK: Tell these men, I had nothing to do with it.

BULL: He registered as John Doe.

NOWAK: John Doe, that's what he said his name was. Came in on Friday night, said he needed a room for one week. Came for the Exposition, he said, to sell souvenirs. But I had my doubts.

FOSTER: You did?

NOWAK: I have a sense of these things, so I made him pay the twelve dollars up front. But I had no idea about this, I've got nothing to do with this insect.

BULL: Walkowiak, the night clerk, said he had a chat with Mr. Doe late one night. [*Pause*] Is that right, Mr. Doe? [*Pause*] He told me your name isn't really John Doe.

WASHBURN: That don't surprise me.

BULL: He said you were a Polish Jew, is that right? [*Pause*] And you were afraid if Mr. Nowak found that out, you might not get a room.

NOWAK: Not at my place, no sir.

BULL: You told him your name was Nieman, Fred Nieman.

NOWAK: Walkowiak said that?

BULL: Tell us about yourself, Mr. Nieman.

FOSTER: Let's hear you talk again.

CZOLGOSZ: Nieman, I am not Nieman. I am nobody.

BULL: We've had enough of this routine.

NOWAK: Tell these men, please, I had nothing to do with it. I had no idea what you were planning to do. All I did was give you a room, tell these men.

CZOLGOSZ [*calmly*]: My name is Leon Czolgosz.

[*Pause*]

BULL: Copy this down.

WASHBURN: Could you spell that?

CZOLGOSZ: I am twenty-eight years old. I was born in Detroit, but lately I am from Cleveland, Ohio. [*Pause*] I killed the President because it was my duty, because he was a tyrant. [*Pause*] Nobody told me to do it, nobody helped me. I did this all by myself, out of duty to my fellow Americans, out of love for my country. I killed him and I don't regret it. [*Pause*] I have nothing else to say. What I did speaks for itself.

BULL: Who else is involved in this?

FOSTER: Where did you get the gun?

CZOLGOSZ: I've got nothing else to say.

FOSTER: How long have you been plotting this?

WASHBURN: Could you spell that for me?

CZOLGOSZ: C–Z–O–L–G–O–S–Z. Czolgosz. And no more.

[*Blackout*]

Scene Seven

[HANNA *and* IDA *stand at the foot of* MCKINLEY's *bed.*]

HANNA: Now, Ida . . . be strong.

[HANNA *leads* IDA, *who moves with difficulty, to a chair beside the bed, near the President's head.*]

HANNA: I'll be right outside.

[HANNA *leaves and* IDA *gently kisses her husband on the forehead, like a mother would her child.*]

IDA: My precious.
MCKINLEY: Is that you?
IDA: I'm right here, my precious.
MCKINLEY: I'm so sorry.
IDA: Shhhh.
MCKINLEY: I'm so very sorry.
IDA: I'm right here.
MCKINLEY: Are you all right?
IDA: I'm just fine.
MCKINLEY: Are you feeling all right?
IDA: Shhhh.

[*She cradles his head in her arms and hums a simple melody for a few moments. Then silence.*]

MCKINLEY: Ida?
IDA: I'm right here, my precious.
MCKINLEY: Are you all right?
IDA: I'm just fine.

[*Silence.* IDA *begins to hum again. Blackout.*]

Scene Eight

[PAUL CZOLGOSZ *sits in a rocking chair, dejected. He's stocky and powerfully built, but now looks on the verge of collapse. A newspaperman,* ARTHUR HAMILTON, *stands beside him, taking notes.*]

HAMILTON: His mother is dead?

PAUL: Yes.

HAMILTON: When did she die?

PAUL: When he was a boy, a young boy.

HAMILTON: That must have upset him.

PAUL: Yes.

[*Pause*]

HAMILTON: I hear you're a socialist.

PAUL: No, not me.

HAMILTON: You let some socialists use the room above your grocery store for their meetings. That's what your neighbor said.

PAUL: I was curious, that's all.

HAMILTON: Did you vote in the last election?

PAUL: I'm no socialist. I vote for McKinley.

HAMILTON [*writing that down*]: For McKinley . . . huh.

PAUL: Leon was not well . . . has not been well the past two years, three years. He quit his job.

HAMILTON: Why'd he do that?

PAUL: Because he was not well. He quit his job at the mill and went to live on our farm, a small farm outside Cleveland I have, in Warrensville. For two years there, he do nothing.

HAMILTON: That was okay with you?

PAUL: I felt he was not well. My wife –

HAMILTON: You got another one?

PAUL: Yes. She said he's just lazy, up to no good. She wanted to kick him out. But I said no, he's a good boy.

HAMILTON: Was he ever in trouble with the law, ever arrested?

PAUL: No, he's a good boy, always go to church, never in trouble.

HAMILTON: Never broke someone's window, never stole anything?

PAUL: Never.

HAMILTON: Did you have any idea he was planning to do this?

PAUL: Oh, no. Oh, my goodness, no. If I had, if I had any idea, I would have stopped him right away myself. He just stay at the farm, sleeping all the time, reading, reading too much, staying in his room all day, away from the rest of the family. [*Pause*] Then he started to make trips.

HAMILTON: Trips? To where?

PAUL: I don't know. Sometimes Cleveland, I think. I don't know. He wouldn't say. He would just go.

HAMILTON: Did he ever bring home any suspicious-looking friends?

PAUL: No. No friends.

HAMILTON: Didn't he have any friends?

PAUL: At work, maybe, but not after that. He keep to himself.

HAMILTON: Any young ladies?

PAUL: Never.

HAMILTON: No sweetheart?

PAUL: Never.

HAMILTON: Huh.

[*Pause*]

PAUL: May I say something?

HAMILTON: Why, sure.

PAUL: I would like to say something. [*Pause*] I love this country. I love it here more than I can say. I love it from a distance and I love it more than ever once I'm here with my family. This is the best country in the world. [*Pause*] If I knew this would happen, if I knew my son would do something like this, I would have stayed in Poland. I would not come here at all.

HAMILTON: Well, it's a little late to be thinking about that.

PAUL: I would never do anything to hurt this country.

HAMILTON: I understand.

PAUL: I would rather we stay in Poland.

HAMILTON: Now I heard from someone that Czolgosz, the word itself, is derived from a Polish verb, which means to drag, creep or crawl.

PAUL: That is not true.

HAMILTON: I heard it from someone at the Immigration Office, from their official interpreter of Polish and Bohemian languages.

PAUL: I don't care.

HAMILTON: And as a noun, he said, it means a creeping, crawling thing, like a snake.

PAUL: That is absolutely false.

[*Blackout*]

Scene Nine

[CZOLGOSZ *sits in his cell, guarded by* WASHBURN. *After a moment,* BULL *enters, followed by* HAMILTON.]

BULL: Hello, Washburn.

WASHBURN: Hello, sir.

BULL: Hello, Leon. How are we today?

[*Pause. No reply.*]

BULL: I've got a man with me who'd like to meet you. Arthur Hamilton, of the *New York Tribune*, this is Washburn.

WASHBURN: Pleased to meet you.

[*They shake hands.*]

BULL: And this is Leon Czolgosz.

[HAMILTON *extends his hand and forces a grin, but* CZOLGOSZ *ignores him.*]

BULL: Leon, Mr. Hamilton would –

CZOLGOSZ: I was wondering if I could get some new clothes.

[*They notice that his white shirt is still spattered with the President's blood. Pause.*]

BULL: I'll see what I can do.

CZOLGOSZ: Thank you.

BULL: Now, Leon, Mr. Hamilton wants to ask you a few questions about what you did and I told him that was fine with me.

CZOLGOSZ: Sorry, but I've got nothing more to say about that.

HAMILTON: People want to know why you did it.

CZOLGOSZ: Let them see for themselves.

HAMILTON: Everyone's interested in your story. [*Pause*] The whole country's talking about you, wondering what you're really like. [*Pause*] People want to know all about you.

BULL: Why'd you do it, Leon?

HAMILTON: Why did you shoot the President?

CZOLGOSZ: I killed the President because it was my duty, because he was a tyrant. I said that already, and on that subject, I've got nothing else to say.

[*Long pause*]

BULL: Leon, you didn't kill anybody. The President's doing just fine.

CZOLGOSZ: I don't believe you.

HAMILTON: Oh, it's true. The doctors say he'll be back to work in a month or so.

[*Pause*]

BULL: Sorry to disappoint you, son.

[*Pause*]

HAMILTON: Do you ever read the papers?

CZOLGOSZ: Huh?

HAMILTON: The newspapers. Got a favorite?

CZOLGOSZ: I don't know, I'm tired.

HAMILTON: You like the Hearst papers? William Randolph Hearst?

CZOLGOSZ: I don't like any of them.

HAMILTON: But you read them.

CZOLGOSZ: Sure, I read them.

HAMILTON: A few weeks ago, Hearst wrote an editorial that said now let me read it to you ... [*He finds it in one of h* *pockets, then reads*] "If bad institutions and bad men ca only be got rid of by killing, then the killing must be done. [*Pause*] Did you happen to come across that?

CZOLGOSZ: I don't know, I'm tired. I don't want to talk.

HAMILTON: Try to remember. Did that influence you?

CZOLGOSZ: No.

HAMILTON: Are you sure?

CZOLGOSZ: I'm sure. [*Pause*] Nobody influenced me.

HAMILTON: Who influenced you, Leon? Somebody must hav influenced you.

CZOLGOSZ: I influenced myself.

HAMILTON: Are you an anarchist?

CZOLGOSZ: I'm an American.

WASHBURN: Oh, Jesus.

CZOLGOSZ: A good American.

HAMILTON: Emma Goldman, did she influence you?

CZOLGOSZ: Thomas Jefferson influenced me. You can't arres him, he's dead.

HAMILTON: People want to know why you did it.

CZOLGOSZ: I listened to the words of the Founding Father that's all.

HAMILTON: I'm not sure I follow you.

CZOLGOSZ: Brutus influenced me, you want to arrest him? Go t Rome and arrest his bones.

HAMILTON: Now, you said McKinley's a ... tyrant. Most peopl don't think so. They just re-elected him by a very wide margin

CZOLGOSZ: What do most people know? They only know wha

you let them know, what you tell them. This President of yours could burp, and you'd write it up the next day as the most brilliant thing anyone's said since Gettysburg.

BULL: Calm down.

CZOLGOSZ: The American people have no idea what is happening right now to their country. Believe me, if my fellow Americans knew what I know, they would do their duty the same as me, and make the same sacrifice. Nearly every one of them would.

HAMILTON: Your father said you quit your job because you weren't feeling well. Were you sick or were you faking it?

[*Pause*]

CZOLGOSZ: When did he say that?

HAMILTON: I saw him the other day.

CZOLGOSZ: You did? [*Pause*] How is he?

HAMILTON: He seemed very upset, Leon. Very ashamed. All he could talk about was how ashamed your whole family felt. [*Pause*] Were you sick, or did you quit your job to get involved in some political work?

CZOLGOSZ: Get out of here. I'm tired.

HAMILTON: Emil Schilling said you liked to drop by the Liberty Club and talk politics with him.

BULL: What's this Liberty Club?

HAMILTON: A bunch of Cleveland anarchists. Leon, you remember Schilling; he remembers you. Said he never liked you, never trusted you.

CZOLGOSZ: Well, that's a compliment. What a timid little weasel. Didn't he remind you of one? Every time I saw him I thought that. This man is nothing, I said to myself. All he can do is talk and talk and talk. Squeak, like a weasel.

HAMILTON: Who else is involved with this? Emma Goldman? Some of the Patterson anarchists?

CZOLGOSZ: Did my father tell you where I worked?

HAMILTON: Yes, he did.

CZOLGOSZ: He told you I quit, but did he tell you where I worked for seven years?

HAMILTON: At a steel mill in Cleveland.

CZOLGOSZ: Steel wire, not steel, that's what I made, for six dollars a week – not enough to keep Rockefeller in cigars. Did my father tell you about the time we went on strike?

HAMILTON: No, but that's not what –

CZOLGOSZ: We went on strike because we were working ten hours a day, six days a week, and we thought, that's not fair. Eight hours a day is what we asked for.

HAMILTON: So you were a union man?

CZOLGOSZ: Sure, you can call me that. I joined this union at my factory, we all did. Then we all went on strike, then we all got fired. Every single one of us, locked out. I was a union man until there was no more union.

HAMILTON: That's a sad story, Leon, but –

CZOLGOSZ: I don't think you heard my story. Did you hear what I just said?

HAMILTON: Schilling said you were a socialist for a while.

CZOLGOSZ: I don't think you heard me. Did you hear what I said?

HAMILTON: Yes.

CZOLGOSZ: You ever worked for a living?

HAMILTON: I've been with the *Tribune* for over twenty-two years.

CZOLGOSZ: I mean work, real work, you ever done any?

HAMILTON: Why'd you quit your job? To join some secret anarchist society?

CZOLGOSZ: I decided to retire, that's all.

HAMILTON: Uh-huh.

[*Pause*]

CZOLGOSZ: You speak any German?

HAMILTON: No, I don't.

CZOLGOSZ: You know how to say "nobody" in German?

HAMILTON: Why don't you tell me.

CZOLGOSZ: Nieman. [*Pause*] That's who I was. [*Pause*] After the strike, I got my old job back, they needed a few men who knew what they were doing. But the foreman made me take a new name. Couldn't have strikers on the payroll.

HAMILTON: Nieman, huh?

CZOLGOSZ: That's right. But I didn't like it, the whole situation. I didn't like the choice every nobody has to face: become a robber or get robbed. So I decided it was time to retire.

HAMILTON: Your father said you quit because you didn't feel well. Said you cried a lot.

CZOLGOSZ: He said that?

HAMILTON: Everything made you cry.

CZOLGOSZ: He didn't say that.

HAMILTON: You don't look like the sensitive type to me.

CZOLGOSZ: Get out of here, I'm tired.

HAMILTON: I think you got involved in some political work.

CZOLGOSZ: Who cares what you think?

HAMILTON: Don't you want everyone to know why you did it?

CZOLGOSZ: You don't hear a word I say.

HAMILTON: Leon, people want to know about you.

CZOLGOSZ: Get out.

[*Pause*]

HAMILTON: I think we can help one another. [*Pause*] The President's going to be all right, and then what was the point? [*Pause*] Everyone wants to know your story. [HAMILTON *and* BULL *rise to leave*] Well, nice talking to you.

BULL: See you, Leon.

[*They start to go.*]

CZOLGOSZ: Get me a newspaper.

[HAMILTON *pulls one from his valise and hands it to* LEON, *who snaps it open and begins to read. Blackout.*]

Scene Ten

[HAMILTON *and* BULL *stand drinking at a bar.*]

HAMILTON: I don't know, I just don't know.

BULL: Oh, it's frightening.

HAMILTON: I lie awake at night and I think, what is this world coming to?

BULL: I don't know.

HAMILTON: What is this world coming to?

BULL: Don't ask me.

HAMILTON: We sent a man to Paris a few years ago, at the height of the bombings there – and the stories he told, Christ you wouldn't believe. Bombs at railway stations, bombs at cafés, women and children blown to bits, these anarchists didn't give a damn. Couldn't care less about innocent bystanders. There are no innocents, they said, to hell with every one of you.

BULL: Good Lord.

HAMILTON: I was afraid of this.

BULL: But this is America, you think. It won't happen here.

HAMILTON: I've got two young daughters, and I follow the news and I wonder what the hell this world is coming to. Lunatics setting off bombs and now this.

BULL: Not in America, oh no, that's everyone's assumption.

HAMILTON: I looked straight into his eyes and I saw . . . something, I don't know, something not quite human.

BULL: He's a hard one, all right.

HAMILTON: I'd call him a worm, but that's an insult to worms. He's as low as you can go in the animal kingdom, a protozoa, some stinking fungus.

BULL: Well, you're doing us a great favor.

HAMILTON: Oh –

BULL: You are, yes you are.

HAMILTON: I bet he loves to rant and rave.

BULL: Not to us. Wouldn't say a thing to us.

HAMILTON: Trust me, he's an anarchist. They hate all politicians, but, oh, how they love to give speeches.

BULL: Just keep him going.

HAMILTON: All right.

BULL: Anything about his motives, his movements that day, any little thing, just keep him going.

HAMILTON: All right.

BULL: I don't think he had any help. But we need to make sure.

HAMILTON: Of course.

[*Pause*]

BULL: Hope I can return the favor. Somehow.

HAMILTON: I think I'm going to make him an offer.

BULL: Whatever you please, that's your business.

[*Pause*]

HAMILTON: You know there's plenty of opportunity left in this country.

BULL: There sure is.

HAMILTON: This is still the land of plenty.

BULL: My boy's in Oregon on five hundred acres, and not a neighbor for miles.

HAMILTON: That's what I mean.

BULL: About the same age, too.

HAMILTON: This is still the land of plenty, long as you're not too lazy or too stupid.

BULL: There's too many folks crammed into these big cities.

HAMILTON: Now there's your problem.

BULL: Thousands and thousands of people, piled right on top each other.

HAMILTON: It's a crime. I think it's criminal. Sometimes, in New York, I feel like I'm in a foreign country. Nobody speaks English!

BULL: I hear there's lots of children going hungry, sleeping four or five to a bed.

HAMILTON: If they've got a bed!

BULL: Good Lord.

HAMILTON: Most of them sleep on the floor, curled up like dogs, little puppydogs. It's a national disgrace, and something better be done before it's too late. [*Pause*] We don't need any more of the Old World's filth floating over here.

BULL: I'm not so sure —

HAMILTON: We should shut the gates, once and for all. We should shut the goddamn gates.

[*Blackout*]

Scene Eleven

[CZOLGOSZ *sits in his cell, looking bruised and dejected.* WASHBURN *enters with* PAUL CZOLGOSZ.]

WASHBURN: Got an old Polack here wants to see you.

PAUL: Look at his face.

WASHBURN: Ugly, huh?

PAUL: Look what you did to his face.

WASHBURN: Oh, he must've tripped and fell down.

[WASHBURN *leaves.*]

PAUL: How do you feel?

CZOLGOSZ: I'm all right.

PAUL: Is it broken, is anything broken?

CZOLGOSZ: I said I'm all right.

[PAUL *examines his face.*]

CZOLGOSZ: Just bruises.

PAUL: Did you lose a tooth? How many did you lose?

[CZOLGOSZ *pulls away from his father. Silence.* PAUL *stares at his son's blood-spattered clothes, then turns away.*]

PAUL: You know, your brothers are changing their name.

CZOLGOSZ: It's about time.

PAUL: Out of the shame they feel. Out of disgrace.

CZOLGOSZ: What about you?

PAUL: This is my name all my life, I told them, and my father's name before that. I will not change it because of my son. [*Pause*] I cannot understand what you did.

CZOLGOSZ: You can't?

PAUL: No, no, I can't. I ask myself over and over, day and night since you did this, how could you be so stupid, and I beg Jesus give the President back his health.

CZOLGOSZ: Save your breath.

PAUL: I pray and pray all week, and now I am happy the President is feeling better, because now you will have time to think about what you did. Seven or eight years, these men tell me, for you to think about how stupid you were, and then maybe you will grow up, maybe you will stop being a baby.

CZOLGOSZ: How about the missus, she changing her name?

PAUL: You should thank her.

CZOLGOSZ: For what?

PAUL [*whispers*]: Soon as Walt tell her what you did, he hear from the neighbor, she got all those books from your room, before any police or newspapermen are there, and she put them in the wagon, and she took them to the quarry, make a big pile and set them on fire.

CZOLGOSZ: She did?

PAUL: Yes, those books always scare her.

CZOLGOSZ: She can go to hell.

PAUL: Shame on you. It's good nobody find them.

CZOLGOSZ: Thank her for nothing.

PAUL: She always said you were weak and stupid and now I think so too.

CZOLGOSZ: To hell with her.

PAUL: Lazy, weak and spoiled. That's what she said.

[*Pause*]

CZOLGOSZ: So you don't like what I did?

PAUL: No, how could I?

CZOLGOSZ: You think it was wrong?

PAUL: Worse than wrong, stupid.

CZOLGOSZ: You never killed anybody?

PAUL: Never.

CZOLGOSZ: Oh. [*Pause*] That's not what I heard.

PAUL: I don't care what you heard. I never have and I never would.

CZOLGOSZ: I heard you once killed a man.

PAUL: So you heard this? From who?

CZOLGOSZ: Walt told me.

PAUL: I don't care what he told you. I'm telling you: no, I never did. So don't accuse me.

[*Long pause*]

CZOLGOSZ: How is Thorstein?

PAUL: Thorstein is fine.

CZOLGOSZ: Does he miss me?

PAUL: Yes. He is the only one.

CZOLGOSZ: Is Sophie taking care of him?

PAUL: No, I am. She won't even pet him.

CZOLGOSZ: Why not?

PAUL: She won't pet him.

CZOLGOSZ: Guess I'm never going to see him again.

PAUL: He's old, but you'll see him.

CZOLGOSZ: He misses me?

PAUL: Yes, at night he's upset. Now he sleeps with us.

CZOLGOSZ: If you come again, or if Walt comes, try to bring him.

PAUL: Walt will not come.

[*Pause*]

CZOLGOSZ: The police were at the house?

PAUL: Yes, every day a new one. And newspapermen, like flies. One man try to take pictures of your room, so I come with a shovel.

CZOLGOSZ: What do you tell them?

PAUL: Who?

CZOLGOSZ: Newspapermen, the police.

PAUL: Whatever they ask, I tell them. [*Pause*] Except the books, a few things.

CZOLGOSZ: You say I was sick?

PAUL: I don't know your secrets, so I can't tell them any.

CZOLGOSZ: What do you tell them?

PAUL: Why?

CZOLGOSZ: You say I was sick?

PAUL: Yes, I tell them you were sick and now I see how sick.

CZOLGOSZ: You have no right to tell them that.

PAUL: You should worry about something else, you should worry about why you did this, and not what I say.

CZOLGOSZ: I don't want you telling people I was sick. This is my business, and if anyone gives explanations, it should be me.

PAUL: I will say what I like.

[*Pause*]

CZOLGOSZ: Remember when we walked home from Northfield, after that big storm?

PAUL: What?

CZOLGOSZ: Years ago, you remember?

PAUL: Yes, you were a little boy.

CZOLGOSZ: It took us hours to get home, and the air was cool and still, and we never said a word, the whole time. We just walked along together, past all those trees that were blown down, through a lot of mud and puddles. And I remember thinking, Poppa knows what I'm feeling. We're feeling exactly the same. I can just point over there or give him a look and he'll know what I mean.

PAUL: That was a big storm.

CZOLGOSZ: And right now I could sit here and look at your face from two feet away and talk for hours – and you still wouldn't understand a thing, not a goddamn thing.

PAUL: Please, not now.

CZOLGOSZ: You have no right to talk to these people about me because you don't know what you're talking about.

PAUL: I know this – no one will come into my store. I know this – I cannot walk out of my own house to the street. I would just as soon stay inside it for the rest of my life. Don't tell me, because I know many things you don't know. [*Pause*] Your sister, ever since this happened, she will not speak your name. In six days, a week now, Sophie has not said your name once. Not one time. And when someone starts to speak about this, about what you did, she gets up and leaves the room. Calmly, she goes, with no fuss. [*Silence*] I have some money for you.

CZOLGOSZ: Keep it.

PAUL: You may need some money for things.

CZOLGOSZ: Keep it, there's nothing here I want to buy.

PAUL: You may need –

CZOLGOSZ: I want you to keep your money. I won't be needing it.

PAUL: All right then, all right. [*Pause*] Do you have a lawyer?

CZOLGOSZ: No.

PAUL: What are you going to do for a lawyer?

CZOLGOSZ: Nothing.

PAUL: You should be thinking of this before, not afterwards. You should find a good lawyer before you go ahead and do anything, because he'll tell you not to do it.

CZOLGOSZ: Is that what you do?

PAUL: What?

CZOLGOSZ: I was in the kitchen one day, making some lunch, and I asked Walt to hand me a knife, to cut a piece of ham with. The knife with the black handle. [*Pause*] Well, he gave me the handle but kept hold of the blade for a second and said, do you know where this knife's been? I didn't know what he was talking about.

PAUL: Lies.

CZOLGOSZ: This's been in a man's gut, he said. Poppa stuck this knife all the way in a man's gut one night.

PAUL: Stupid lies.

CZOLGOSZ: That's just what I said. But Walt kept insisting it was the truth, so we found your brother, and we asked him. And when he said, sit down, boys, I nearly passed out. I thought Walt was just fictionalizing again. Then your brother told us the whole story, about how this was an evil man, a criminal, and you had no choice. He wanted us to know how brave you'd been, how you did it for our sake, and then he made us swear never to tell a soul. [*Pause*] From then on, I couldn't go anywhere near that knife. I was scared to death, just to see it sitting on the counter.

PAUL: I don't know what you're talking about.

CZOLGOSZ: The same knife you'd carve turkeys with.

[*Pause*]

PAUL: If you think what I did and what you did are the same, you're out of your mind.

CZOLGOSZ: You sound ashamed.

PAUL: What I did was wrong and what you did was stupid and in a few years you'll grow up and see that it's true.

[*Blackout*]

Scene Twelve

[IDA *and* HANNA *sit in chairs beside the President's bed. Hanna's nephew,* CLARK, *a young man in a Navy uniform, stands at the foot of the bed. The President appears weak, but his voice sounds clear and strong.*]

MCKINLEY: Do everything the best you know how, and if you are in doubt, ask your superior officer the best way to do it. Be careful about your writing. See that your words are spelled correctly. Better keep a little pocket dictionary with you. It mars an official paper or letter to have a word misspelled. Look after your diet, take no intoxicants, indulge in no immoral practices. Keep both your life and your speech clean, and be brave. Try always to be brave on behalf of your country.

CLARK: I will, sir.

MCKINLEY: You'll do fine, I'm sure of it.

IDA: Your parents must be so proud.

HANNA: His mother wants to go with him, but the Captain said no!

CLARK: I said no.

MCKINLEY: Ida, perhaps you and the boy would like to get some fresh air in the garden.

IDA: That sounds nice.

MCKINLEY: I need a few words with Mark before he goes.

IDA: No politics.

MCKINLEY: No politics.

IDA: Mr. Hanna?

HANNA: I promise.

CLARK: I'll always remember your words, Mr. President. I wish you the best of health. [*He salutes.*]

MCKINLEY: It's been a pleasure.

[IDA *takes* CLARK'S *arm.*]

IDA: Have you got a sweetheart?

CLARK: As a matter of fact, I'm engaged.

IDA: You must write to her every day.

[IDA *and* CLARK *leave.*]

HANNA: I can still cancel my trip.

MCKINLEY: No, no, no. Bring my greetings to the G.A.R. There's nothing for you to do here.

HANNA: Are you sure?

MCKINLEY: Absolutely. Life must go on. [*Pause*] Your nephew seems like a fine young man.

HANNA: He is, but thank God he enlisted. You know he just graduated from Yale near the top of his class.

MCKINLEY: That's right, he's a college man.

HANNA: We're hoping the Navy will knock a lot of the Yale out of him.

MCKINLEY: Some practical experience will do him good.

[*Pause*]

HANNA: Guess you want to hear about the reciprocity bill. Soon as I'm back in Washington, I'll have the boys draw something up and we'll get it to the Senate right away.

MCKINLEY: That sounds fine.

HANNA: The way people are feeling, it'll pass in the blink of an eye. Right now we could pass a bill moving Christmas to the middle part of August.

MCKINLEY: Oh, no.

HANNA: Yes, we could. Now, I'm not saying we should cash in on all this outpouring of sympathy. That is not what I'm saying. But we should certainly take advantage of the situation, within limits, of course. We should make the best of this damn business.

MCKINLEY: We can discuss this another time.

HANNA: Lodge thinks we might even be able to push through –

MCKINLEY: Another time, Mark. [*Pause*] There are other things on my mind. Important things . . . of a personal nature.

HANNA: Is there anything I can do?

MCKINLEY: This isn't easy for me to say. This is difficult for me.

HANNA: You know, anything I can do –

MCKINLEY: Yes.

HANNA: I'll do without question.

MCKINLEY: I know, and I appreciate it.

HANNA: Anything.

[*Pause*]

MCKINLEY: Mark, I look upon you as my dearest friend in the world.

HANNA: Oh –

MCKINLEY: Yes, I do, and it's time I said so.

HANNA: It's an honor, the greatest honor.

MCKINLEY: You and I have discussed so many things close to my heart over the years, everything under the sun. [*Pause*] But I've never spoken to you about Ida, not really. I've never spoken to anyone about my true feelings for her. Never in my whole life.

HANNA: You have my complete confidence.

MCKINLEY: I have no doubt about that. [*Pause*] This is difficult for me. There are things I've never discussed with anyone. It's not in my nature. [*Pause*] Should my injury prove fatal –

HANNA: Oh, baloney, you look healthier than I do!

MCKINLEY: Should my injury prove fatal, I would like Ida under the best possible care . . . and I wonder whether you would arrange things.

HANNA: Why, of course, but –

MCKINLEY: This is a great responsibility, not something to be taken lightly.

HANNA: Of course.

MCKINLEY: She is my whole life. People haven't realized this. People who've known me for many years, they haven't taken the time to understand this. I wish you could have seen Ida when we first met. I wish you could have seen her.

Ida was the life of every party. She simply sparkled. When she walked into a room full of people, the whole room suddenly felt different, full of electricity, everyone brightened up. People in Canton couldn't get enough of her.

HANNA: That's what I've heard.

MCKINLEY: It's the truth. Mark, she's the most sensitive creature on this earth. Most people would never have survived what she's been through. Or if they did, it would only be because they're insensitive, because they don't feel a thing. Well, Ida feels too much. That's the cross she's had to bear. She simply feels too much.

HANNA: I've always adored Ida.

MCKINLEY: I've never spoken to anyone about this. It's not in my nature. And it's hurt me, more than I can express, to think that some people look upon her as a pathetic invalid. I know they do. They think she's been a drain on my energies, when the truth is, she's the strongest person I've ever met. She is my whole life.

HANNA: You have my word that Charlotte and I will look after Ida, if need be, as though she were a member of our own family – which is how we think of her. Please, say no more.

MCKINLEY: There are a number of things you ought to know.

HANNA: Whatever's appropriate.

[*Blackout*]

Scene Thirteen

[HAMILTON, BULL *and* WASHBURN *sit with* CZOLGOSZ *in his cell.*]

CZOLGOSZ [*for posterity*]: Rome was a virtuous little republic once. Humble farmers working the land with their families, a healthy people. Then vanity did them in. A few Romans got rich and decided they wanted to boss everyone else around. The farmers were driven into debt and then thrown off their land. Mobs gathered in Rome, these once proud farmers now lived in wretched poverty, and now they were ready to throw their lot in with any corrupt politician who promised them more bread and circuses. Instead of working for a living, Rome decided to conquer other peoples, plunder their lands, steal their treasures, and live off them. Now the Romans were the bigshot rulers of the world, and they acted like it. Their virtuous little republic had become a mighty empire, had grown rotten with luxury and every vice you can imagine. Vanity – their vanity did them in, and then they had to pay the price. One day the Visigoths swept into town, raped, pillaged and burned Rome to the ground. [*Pause*] Nothing but ruins there now.

HAMILTON: It's too bad, isn't it?

CZOLGOSZ: That's how it works and that's how it always works. Right now, England is the big banker and the big bully of the world, but just you wait. Soon they'll pay the price for their British Empire of greed and conquest and crime.

HAMILTON: Enough history for now.

CZOLGOSZ: You need to know this.

HAMILTON: Oh, I've read a little about Rome.

CZOLGOSZ: But did you learn anything from it? Did you understand a single thing?

HAMILTON: Why did you shoot the President, Leon?

CZOLGOSZ: It's not just a bunch of old stories. It's your country, it's your life at stake.

HAMILTON: Why did you shoot the President? That's what I'd like to know.

CZOLGOSZ: Five thousand American boys dead in the Philippines, that's why.

HAMILTON: Is that why you did it?

CZOLGOSZ: A hundred thousand Filipinos slaughtered on their own land by Americans, that's why.

HAMILTON: So this was a protest.

CZOLGOSZ: No, this wasn't a protest. Lots of people protested against McKinley's bloody war of conquest, and it didn't do a damn thing. You can't stop a train wreck from happening by protesting against it. You've got to do something drastic, shoot the engineer.

HAMILTON: You shot a nice man in the gut, Leon.

CZOLGOSZ: Nice man? Is this President of yours a nice man?

HAMILTON: One of the nicest. I've met a lot of politicians in my day, and as a rule, I don't care for them. William McKinley, why, a man like that appears only once in a century. A good man, through and through, with a truly noble character. That's who you shot.

CZOLGOSZ: Well, these nice men, they're usually the biggest murderers.

BULL: Have some decency.

CZOLGOSZ: The biggest murderers and the biggest cowards.

WASHBURN: And what about you? Shooting an unarmed man as he shakes your hand?

CZOLGOSZ: Well, I did what I did for everyone to see. I looked the President in the eye before I shot him in the gut. These nice men, oh, they're the worst. They can slaughter thousands, just by signing a piece of paper. It's that easy for them, no mess. This President of yours, he sits in his comfortable chair, sunshine streaming in the window, birds chirping outside, and with a fancy pen, he signs a piece of paper, then goes out for brandy and a cigar. A piece of paper – you could cut your finger on it, maybe, but it sure doesn't look like something that could kill you. Well, this piece of paper of his starts multiplying into more pieces of paper, into all kinds of orders, directives, commands. And then, like magic, these pieces of paper turn into solid things, real things, into real life. Now warships raise anchor and set sail for foreign ports. The wheels are set in motion. No more planning, no more practicing, the game-playing is over. Guns get loaded, cannons are raised, the enemy is spotted, now ready, aim, FIRE. [*Pause*]

Meanwhile, the President kisses his wife, says isn't it lovely out, and goes for a stroll in the rose garden. Halfway across the world, his piece of paper is making widows and orphans by the thousand, but the President doesn't get a drop of blood on his soft, flabby hands. Nice men rarely do. Later in the day, there's some more pieces of paper to sign. And later that night, the President doesn't toss and turn, thinking about blood and gore and pieces of arms and legs. No, he just lies there on his back like a beached whale – and snores.

HAMILTON: The President does all that?

CZOLGOSZ: That's right.

HAMILTON: The President does it, nobody else? Not the Congress that passed the law, not the millions of people that cast their vote?

CZOLGOSZ: Don't try to confuse things. The President does whatever he wants to do, lets people know later, and then makes them think that's what they wanted all along.

HAMILTON: You hold the President personally to blame for –

CZOLGOSZ: He signs the pieces of paper, don't he?

[*Pause*]

HAMILTON: Leon, you've got no regrets about what you did?

CZOLGOSZ: Oh, I wish I were a better shot.

HAMILTON: Not a doubt in your mind?

CZOLGOSZ: Nope. I had a few doubts, but they passed.

BULL: When was that?

CZOLGOSZ: Opening day, I had my gun with me. I was going to shoot McKinley on opening day, right after he switched on those lights.

BULL: Why didn't you?

CZOLGOSZ: He was too far away, lots of people were pushing against me. So I waited and listened to his speech – what a fucking bore that was – and I looked at all the fancy electric lights. I just stared at those lights, thinking about how awful they were. Pink and blue lights? Who needs them? You can have all the electric lights in the world, and still not see a damn thing.

HAMILTON: I think we're straying.

CZOLGOSZ: If that's the future, I don't mind missing it. [*Pause*] Well, I got myself to the spot where McKinley's carriage was waiting. After he was done blabbing away, I had a clear shot and then someone stepped in front of me for a second. Then I saw two men in fancy suits – and I couldn't tell the difference between them. I was less than ten feet, maybe eight feet away from them, and I couldn't tell which one was McKinley and which one was just another flunky. Well, that threw me for a loop. It did. So I just stood there and watched that carriage drive away.

BULL: You stood there alone, there was nobody with you?

CZOLGOSZ: Like I said, I was surrounded by people, everywhere, but I was on my own.

HAMILTON: Then what did you do?

CZOLGOSZ: Oh, I wandered around the Exposition, wondering what the hell to do. Two fat old men, one's President of the U.S.A., the other's God only knows who, somebody's uncle, but you can't tell them apart. They look exactly the same, ordinary folks like you and me – except fatter. I didn't know what to do, that threw me. Later I ate some Chinese stuff at the big Pagoda and watched the fireworks show. Did you see that?

HAMILTON: I was in New York.

CZOLGOSZ: It was something. Right, Mr. Bull? You must have seen it.

BULL: Oh, it was something.

CZOLGOSZ: A bunch of little men seeing how big a boom they can make, how loud a bang. That's the whole story in a nut-shell – the whole story. [*Pause*] There was this huge Southern cross in white flames, a shower of pearls, then a tribute to the U.S. Navy. What did you think of that, Mr. Bull?

BULL: Very impressive.

CZOLGOSZ: You're right, but it would've been even more impressive if they'd blown up the real ships instead. There would have been a point to it. Our own battleships are going to sink us. They'll send us straight to the bottom. [*Pause*] And then came the Grand Finale, explosion after explosion, growing bigger and bigger, so loud you thought you'd go deaf, so bright that when one of those things went off, I swear to God, it looked like three in the afternoon. [*Pause*] And then there it was, a gigantic portrait of the President, blazing in all sorts of colors, with a caption beneath his face spelled out across the sky: Welcome . . . McKinley . . . Chief of Our Nation . . . and . . . Our Empire. [*Pause*] Well, that was enough for me.

HAMILTON: The Empire part?

CZOLGOSZ: The whole thing.

HAMILTON: Leon . . . what made you think you could get away with it? How were you planning to escape?

CZOLGOSZ: Escape? Oh no, that was never part of the plan. I thought your President and me would go off together, wherever it is murderers go – to hell or to compost. Escape never entered my mind.

[*Pause*]

HAMILTON: It meant that much to you, this protest?

CZOLGOSZ: Why's that so hard to swallow? A true patriot is always ready to give his life for his country. I'm no different from the brave American boys who died in McKinley's war, except they didn't know any better. They died for no good reason, and now their corpses are rotting away in foreign soil thousands of miles from home.

WASHBURN: I can't listen to any more of this.

BULL: Go outside, then.

[WASHBURN *leaves*.]

HAMILTON: You see yourself as a martyr for liberty.

CZOLGOSZ: Almost a martyr.

HAMILTON: You really do.

CZOLGOSZ: Yes, sir, I do.

HAMILTON: A national hero, some day.

CZOLGOSZ: You never know.

HAMILTON: Some day there'll be a Leon Czolgosz Memorial in Washington, with a statue and a park.

CZOLGOSZ: Sounds funny, huh, but in ancient Greece, when a man killed a tyrant, the people would celebrate him and honor him and build him a shrine.

HAMILTON: This ain't Greece, Leon, and nobody's ever going to dedicate a monument to you. I can promise you that.

CZOLGOSZ: Well, being a hero was hardly the first thing on my mind.

HAMILTON: Then what was? What was first and foremost on your mind?

CZOLGOSZ: My country.

HAMILTON: Oh, I see. America came first, not Leon.

CZOLGOSZ: That's right. This country was supposed to be different.

HAMILTON: You thought you'd change everything by shooting the President. You'd change from Nobody to Somebody.

CZOLGOSZ: This country was supposed to be different, that's what Washington, Jefferson, Madison and Monroe said. They were great men, they were giants, there's nothing but pygmies in office now.

HAMILTON: You'd change everything with two bullets.

CZOLGOSZ: We don't need a standing army, the Founding Fathers said.

HAMILTON: You don't think much of our duty –

CZOLGOSZ: We should mind our own goddamn business and leave other folks alone. You don't help anyone by blowing them to smithereens. You don't help anyone by becoming their boss, don't kid me with that.

HAMILTON: Times change, Leon.

CZOLGOSZ: Some things never change. The first step on the road to empire is the first step toward destruction. One leads to the other sure as night follows day. You may get to feel like a bigshot for a while, but your vanity will lay you low. If America chooses to become the big bully of the world, I promise *you*, America will pay. We will be punished. [*Pause*] And when that awful day comes, when the White House is in flames, and the Capitol's in flames, and the Declaration of Independence is burnt to a little heap of ashes – you'll know why. And you'll know we had it coming to us.

[*Silence*]

HAMILTON: Leon, your family is very upset by what you've done, very ashamed.

[*Pause*]

CZOLGOSZ: I feel bad about that.

HAMILTON: Life wasn't easy for them before.

CZOLGOSZ: I feel bad. They had nothing to do with this.

HAMILTON: There've been some threats from neighbors, local shopkeepers won't let them in their stores, they're being shunned by most of their old friends. People either hate them or are afraid to be seen with them.

CZOLGOSZ: I feel bad about that.

HAMILTON: If you could, would you do something to help them?

BULL: I'll be right outside.

[BULL *leaves. Pause*]

CZOLGOSZ: I don't see what I can do.

HAMILTON: Well, that's what I'd like to discuss. [*Pause*] Now, I think I know why you did it, I think I understand. And I'd like to invite a few other reporters here, somebody from the *World*, somebody from the *Times*, Richard Harding Davis from the *Journal*, if I can get hold of him. And I'd like you to tell them exactly what you told me, everything, including

the business about Rome – but I'd like you to add one
more thing. [*Pause*] Tell them William Randolph Hearst
influenced you to do it, tell them his editorials gave you the
idea, and my paper will make a sizable payment to your
father. [*Pause*] Ten thousand dollars. [*Pause*] More money
than he's seen his entire life. [*Pause*] Think it over, Leon.
He always worked hard for you.

CZOLGOSZ: Tell these reporters Hearst made me do it?

HAMILTON: Say anything you like, but someplace add that.

CZOLGOSZ: I'd rather shoot every one of you in the gut.

[*Blackout*]

Scene Fourteen

[HANNA *and* CLARK *stand with suitcases at a railway
station.*]

CLARK: I thought you were mapping out strategy on the Far East.

HANNA: Nope. We were chatting about Ida McKinley.

CLARK: She's sweet, but a little . . . odd, isn't she?

HANNA: A little?

CLARK: Isn't she?

HANNA: Clark, she's extremely odd. She's a real oddball, completely neurotic, an epileptic as well as a hypochondriac, a
total pain in the ass most of the time, and a sweet gal every
now and then. She's one hell of a mess.

CLARK: I thought so.

HANNA: You've got to admire the President's good nature. He
treats her like a princess, always, like she's royalty. I would
have strangled her years ago.

CLARK: What were you talking about?

HANNA: Oh . . . about a number of things.

CLARK: What's the matter with her?

HANNA: Nerves, that's all. The gal's nerves are shot to hell. Clark,

I consider you an adult now, you're old enough to hear such things.

CLARK: What's she so nervous about?

HANNA: Life, that's all.

CLARK: Life?

HANNA: It's been rough for her. Both her little daughters and her mother died in a period of about two years. Must have been around '73 to '75. Well, that did it to her. Never had children again.

CLARK: Gosh, how awful.

HANNA: Yes, a horrible thing. Now she likes to sit in dark rooms for hours at a time, all by herself. You'll be having a pleasant conversation with her and then, all of a sudden, she'll be weeping for no reason. And a couple of times a week she has fits.

CLARK: Oh my gosh, that's awful.

HANNA: You're old enough to hear these things now. Life can really give you a kick in the teeth. But the President, he's an amazing fellow. In politics you need a lovely lady on your arm to show you're a healthy man, soften things up a bit. Well, he wound up with a neurotic, but overcame the situation, a situation that would have ruined just about anyone else. That's a great man for you.

CLARK: I had no idea.

HANNA: You could learn a thing or two from this, Clark. A thing or two that's useful.

CLARK: What did he do?

HANNA: He did the only thing possible in the situation. His pretty little wife had turned into an oddball, the sort of person you're embarrassed to be seen with in public. He faced a problem, an enormous problem.

CLARK: So, what did he do?

HANNA: Clark, he ignored it, he completely ignored it. He just pretended there was nothing out of the ordinary with this gal! We'd be at a dinner with important people, bankers, senators, judges. Then all of a sudden, right at the table, Ida'd start having a fit. [HANNA *grimaces*] That's what she looks like when she's having a fit. Horrible. And the President, he would simply pull a handkerchief from his pocket . . . [HANNA *pulls out his own handkerchief*] . . . and plop it right over her face. [HANNA *shoves it over* CLARK's *face*] He'd do that without interrupting a sentence, and he'd leave it there until her fit was through. [HANNA *removes the handkerchief.*]

CLARK: My goodness.

HANNA: And because he ignored it, everyone else had to. He just went on with the conversation, as though nothing unusual had happened. You could learn a great deal from the President. He's a remarkable fellow.

CLARK: Thank God he's feeling so much better.

HANNA: Thank God is right.

CLARK: And thank God for Theodore Roosevelt.

HANNA: Don't you dare.

CLARK: I think he's done a marvelous job this week, re-assuring the nation.

HANNA: Oh, is that what you think?

CLARK: You couldn't ask for a better Vice President.

HANNA: Is that how everyone thinks in the Ivy League?

CLARK: I don't know about everyone, but a lot of the fellows think Roosevelt's swell, that he'd make a fine President some day.

HANNA: Your friends must have horseshit for brains.

CLARK: I thought –

HANNA: That man is a threat to the republic. He is a no-good smartass cowboy and the fact that he's just one life away from the Presidency has kept me from getting a wink of sleep all week.

CLARK: I thought you chose him.

HANNA: I would have chosen just about any circus pinhead over Theodore Roosevelt for that job. You cannot do business with the man. He's entirely unreasonable, and this world cannot be run by unreasonable men. They're too dangerous. Now, William McKinley, there is the most reasonable man I have ever met in my life. Everyone loves him for it. If you talk sense to the President, he'll listen to you, and you can be sure he'll do whatever's reasonable, he'll do the reasonable thing. You can't talk sense to Roosevelt. Disagree with Teddy, and he thinks you're trampling all over the American flag, you're a traitor, you're Benedict Arnold, you should be taken outside and shot. You can't talk sense to a bully, because a bully acts from his gut. Roosevelt thinks it's his brain doing the talking, but it's always his gut running the show. What can you say to a man's gut? Nothing. All you can do is wait for the right moment to kick it.

CLARK: I thought you made him Vice President.

HANNA: I most certainly did not. I wouldn't put Teddy to work in the Post Office, because within a month you'd see his goddamn face on every two cent stamp. Platt and Quay wanted him out of New York, they wanted to ruin his career once and for all. I said great, find some floozy whose new-born babe has big buck teeth. That'll ruin him. But that wasn't good enough, they wanted Teddy to fade into obscurity forever. So they made me make him Vice President.

CLARK: I don't believe it.

HANNA: Well, it's the truth unfortunately. The unfortunate truth.

[*A train whistle blows.*]

CLARK: Here's the train.

HANNA: I fought against it but I lost and now I want to hear those two bastards beg my forgiveness, beg for it.

CLARK: This is our train.

HANNA: Just two weeks ago, Teddy stopped by my office to see if I'd go with him to some moving picture show. I said fine, we went to see it, and at one point in the show, this cowboy actor jumps off his horse onto this speeding train, climbs up the side of the dining car, and fights three villains on the roof as the train screams around corners and through tunnels and so on. Finally, this cowboy actor gets knocked off the top while they're tearing across this long bridge over a deep, deep gorge. And somehow, it was amazing, he grabs hold of a beam with one hand on the way down, and just dangles there, in mid-air, way above the creek. Now, I see this and I say to myself, where in hell do they find someone idiotic enough to do something like that. And at that very instant, Teddy turns to me and says, Hanna, that's what I'd want to do if I weren't Vice President. Well, Teddy, I thought to myself, there just might be a career in it for you, once you're finished being Vice President. I didn't say that to him, of course, but I meant it, and I'm hoping for it with all my heart. I'd pay ten cents to see Teddy fall into a gorge. I'd pay ten cents to see it every day for a month.

CLARK: This is our train.

HANNA: Oh, shut up and get on it, then.

[*Blackout*]

Scene Fifteen

[CZOLGOSZ *sits in his cell, guarded by* WASHBURN, *who stands nearby reading a newspaper. After a few moments,* CZOLGOSZ *strains to get a look.* WASHBURN *notices and turns his back.*]

CZOLGOSZ: That the *Tribune*?

WASHBURN: Yup.

CZOLGOSZ: Think I could have a look when you're done?

WASHBURN: Nope.

[*Pause*]

CZOLGOSZ: Anything by that reporter in it?

WASHBURN: Stop bothering me. Can't you see I'm reading?

CZOLGOSZ: Just wondering.

[*Pause*]

WASHBURN: If there was something, why should I tell you? You're big and famous, all right, but I'm not going to help you get any pleasure out of it.

CZOLGOSZ: Just curious.

WASHBURN: There's not a single word about you in this entire paper. [*Long pause*] Well, looky here! There's an article by Mr. Arthur Hamilton.

CZOLGOZ: What's it say?

WASHBURN: That's for me to know.

CZOLGOSZ: Truth is, Washburn, you can't read. You've just been standing there trying to look intelligent.

WASHBURN: "Assassin Confesses to Dastardly Crime." That's what it says.

CZOLGOSZ: Read me the article.

WASHBURN: Oh no.

CZOLGOSZ: It says I confessed, but does it say why?

WASHBURN: Because you're a dumb Polack.

CZOLGOSZ: What does it say?

WASHBURN: Well, let me see here. [*He looks*] Just says you're one of them anarchists.

CZOLGOSZ: That's all?

WASHBURN: [*reads*]: "Emma Goldman's words set my soul on fire." [*Laughs*] Then did you start kissing her?

CZOLGOSZ: Let me see.

[WASHBURN *tosses him the paper.*]

WASHBURN: I've seen Emma Goldman's picture. She's uglier than a mule.

[CZOLGOSZ *skims the article, then returns the paper to* WASHBURN.]

CZOLGOSZ: All yours.

WASHBURN: Oh, don't be upset. If you'd said anything important Mr. Hamilton would've put it in there.

CZOLGOSZ: Just the opposite.

WASHBURN: You're all upset. Well, don't be. Mr. Hamilton saved everyone from the stink of your manure. It was a public service he did.

CZOLGOSZ: The people will suffer now, not me.

WASHBURN: The people? Which people are you talking about? People I know don't want to listen to your shit. They want to get a rope and string you up from the nearest tree. And it's this government you go on about that's saving your neck. They're paying me good money to keep you safe and sound.

CZOLGOSZ: Show a little guts, then, and kill me.

[*Pause*]

WASHBURN: Listen to this. [*Reads*] "Churchgoers Punish Man Who Speaks Against McKinley." [*Pause. Then he reads*] "Fairmont, Nebraska. Church service was interrupted in this small town when a member of the congregation, H. D. Gosser, stood up and said those who prayed for the President's recovery were simply kissing the hand of their oppressor. Gosser said that McKinley was a puppet, and that Mark Hanna, the Trusts, and the Wall Street crowd pulled all the strings. At this point, Gosser was rudely interrupted by a group of young men, who carried him to a small pond a short distance away. There he was repeatedly doused until he nearly drowned. Then he was set astride a rail and paraded through town. Finally, Gosser was dumped in a thicket and everyone returned to church." [*Pause*] Well, good for them. And here's another one. [*Reads again*] "Anarchist Preacher in Indiana Tarred and Feathered."

CZOLGOSZ: That's enough.

WASHBURN: That's what people think of you. You're a failure, Leon, and everybody hates you.

[*Long pause*]

CZOLGOSZ: Ever been to New York City?

WASHBURN: Nope.

CZOLGOSZ: How long've you lived in Buffalo?

WASHBURN: Twenty-seven years, my whole life.

CZOLGOSZ: And you've never been to New York City?

WASHBURN: Nope.

CZOLGOSZ: Not even for a couple of days?

WASHBURN: Never had the desire. [*Pause*] Why'd you ask?

CZOLGOSZ: You remind me of a fellow I met there.

WASHBURN: Yeah?

CZOLGOSZ: Ever hear of Delmonico's?

WASHBURN: Should I've?

CZOLGOSZ: It's the best place in town, where the smart set go every night. At one table, there'll be a Carnegie, at the next one, there'll be a Vanderbilt, near by there's some famous actress and her sister, who's just as pretty, but younger.

WASHBURN: What were you doing in there, washing dishes?

CZOLGOSZ: Oh, I've never been in. But one night I stood outside there for a few hours.

WASHBURN: What's the point of this story, if you've never been inside there?

CZOLGOSZ: There was this huge negro at the door, and they had him decked out in a bright red uniform with shiny gold buttons, and this furry black hat. Like it was some European palace and he was the honor guard. Every time some millionaire walked up, this negro'd smile and open the door. And if he was lucky, they'd give him a nickel as a tip.

WASHBURN: I'm not paying attention.

CZOLGOSZ: That's who you remind me of.

WASHBURN: You're talking to yourself now.

CZOLGOSZ: I understand why he does it. His daddy was probably a slave, and this is a step up. Despite all the humiliation, he's getting paid. Was your daddy a slave?

WASHBURN: Shut up, you dumb Polack.

CZOLGOSZ: Yet here you are, opening and closing doors for the millionaires. Mostly closing them.

WASHBURN: When you get out of here, I hope they send you back to wherever you came from, the dirty little village where you were made.

CZOLGOSZ: I was made in Detroit.

WASHBURN: You're still foreign scum, that's clear as can be.

CZOLGOSZ: I'm more American than you are.

WASHBURN: That's a funny one.

CZOLGOSZ: I was born in America, and raised in America, and what I did I did out of love for America.

WASHBURN: If I can't say a man's last name, then he ain't American. You don't come near passing the test.

CZOLGOSZ: And what are you?

WASHBURN: Oh, I'm an American, nobody argues with that. I was in the Army for this war you get so worked up about.

CZOLGOSZ: Kill anybody?

WASHBURN: Nope. But I would've, if I'd had to. I never made it out of the States, but some friends of mine did, and one of them didn't come back.

CZOLGOSZ: You're not an American if you were in that army.

WASHBURN: One of my very best friends died of flu in Santiago.

CZOLGOSZ: Following orders, wearing a uniform, marching in step with the fellow next to you, that's the exact opposite of being American.

WASHBURN: Don't you tell me what's American and what's not. One of my ancestors was at Valley Forge and another got shot at the Battle of New Orleans, while yours were living in filth and speaking Polack.

CZOLGOSZ: You should try tracing your ancestors even further back. You'll find apes. Big hairy apes. Not that far back, maybe.

WASHBURN: Why, you – [*he grabs* CZOLGOSZ] I ought to kill you right now.

CZOLGOSZ: You don't have the guts.

WASHBURN: I ought to teach you respect.

[WASHBURN *gets* CZOLGOSZ *in a headlock and starts punching him. After a moment,* BULL *arrives, carrying a new suit on a hanger.* WASHBURN, *embarrassed, lets go.* CZOLGOSZ *falls to the floor, and then there's a long pause.*]

BULL: See if this fits.

[*Blackout*]

Scene Sixteen

[IDA *sits beside the President knitting a pink babysuit, while he sits up in bed, watching her.*]

MCKINLEY: Who's that one for?

IDA: For the little Davis girl. Her name's Jean, I think.

MCKINLEY: Gene Davis?

IDA: That's right, precious.

[*Pause*]

MCKINLEY: Ida –

IDA: What, dear?

MCKINLEY: I'm afraid it's little Eugene Davis, named after the uncle.

IDA: Couldn't be, she's a girl.

MCKINLEY: I'm afraid not.

IDA: I met her myself, she's an adorable little girl.

MCKINLEY: I saw Eugene Davis two weeks ago. He's a pal of mine from way back. Got shot at Antietam, walks with a limp. He told me all about his new nephew.

IDA [*drops her knitting*]: Oh my, and look what I've done!

MCKINLEY: It looks lovely.

IDA: I've been wasting my time.

MCKINLEY: There'll be some use for it.

IDA: I don't think so.

MCKINLEY: A lot of our young friends are busy.

IDA: My fingers are aching.

MCKINLEY: Here.

[*He takes her hands and kisses them.*]

IDA: Every one of them aches.

MCKINLEY: Give them a rest.

IDA: I was tired of knitting anyway.

[*Pause*]

MCKINLEY: Darling, I think I'll take a little nap.

IDA: That sounds nice.

MCKINLEY: Doris!

IDA: I think I'll take one, too.

[DORIS *arrives*]

MCKINLEY: Could you see Mrs. McKinley to her room?

[DORIS *helps* IDA *stand.*]

IDA: I'll be back in a few hours.

[*She kisses him on the forehead.*]

MCKINLEY: I look forward to it.

IDA: Sweet dreams, precious.

MCKINLEY: And to you.

[IDA *and* DORIS *leave. The lights dim. Silence. Then* MCKINLEY *rises from his bed, stretches, yawns, and pulls off his nightshirt, while facing the audience, revealing a large, bloody bandage on his chest. He begins to put on a formal suit, and then two* VALETS *appear to help him and*

51

speed up the task. After a moment, an organ begins to play a funeral dirge. The bed is wheeled offstage and an open coffin takes its place. Once he's finished getting dressed, MCKINLEY *faces the audience, solemnly bows, and then, with help from the* VALETS, *climbs into the coffin. An American flag is unfurled, the coffin is closed, the flag is draped over it. A podium is wheeled out, a* REVEREND *ascends it, and the dirge ends. The lights come up on the funeral scene and, simultaneously, on* CZOLGOSZ *sitting alone in his cell. The organ plays softly in the background.*]

REVEREND: Our President is dead. We can hardly believe it. But his spirit shall live on, of that we are certain. So long as this Republic stands for freedom and for liberty, the names of three great men shall never be forgotten. They will be etched forever upon the heart of every American: George Washington, the father of our nation; Abraham Lincoln, the loyal son who kept us one; and William McKinley, who more than any other man, fully embodied the timeless wisdom and the virtues of these United States.

[*Blackout*]

Act II

Scene One

[THEODORE ROOSEVELT *stands behind a podium and gives a speech with tremendous gusto, exhibiting all the power and charisma that* MCKINLEY *lacked, pounding the podium for emphasis.*]

ROOSEVELT: Of the last seven elected Presidents, William McKinley is the third who has been murdered, and this fact should cause grave alarm among all loyal American citizens. Moreover, the circumstances of this assassination have a peculiarly sinister significance. William McKinley was killed by a professed anarchist. The blow was aimed not at this President, but at all Presidents – at every symbol of government. Anarchy is no more an expression of "social discontent" than picking pockets or wife-beating. The anarchist is merely one type of criminal, and his protest of concern for the common workingman is outrageous in its impudent falsity. He is a villain and nothing more. He is, in no shape or way, a "product of social conditions", save as a highwayman is "produced" by the fact that an unarmed man happens to have a purse. [*Pause*] Indeed, anarchy is a crime against the whole human race; and all mankind should band against the anarchist. His creed should be made an offense against the law of nations, like piracy and the slave trade – for it is a crime of blacker infamy than both. Let anarchists and their simple-minded sympathizers be warned: We will not stand for it here. The American people are slow to wrath, but once their wrath is kindled, it burns like a consuming flame.

[*Blackout*]

Scene Two

[CZOLGOSZ *sits on a stool in his prison cell, head in hands, motionless. The lights are dim. After a few moments, the lights go up and* WASHBURN *arrives with* LORAN L. LEWIS, *a tall, thin and elderly man.*]

WASHBURN: Things sinking in, Leon? [*Pause. Then louder*] Leon – there's a lawyer here to see you – Mr. Lewis. [CZOLGOSZ *looks up.*] Now don't act funny. [*To* LEWIS] I'll be just round the corner.

[*Exit* WASHBURN]

LEWIS: My name's Loran L. Lewis.

[CZOLGOSZ *stands, shakes hands.*]

CZOLGOSZ: Nice to meet you. Here, sit down, please. [LEWIS *sits,* CZOLGOSZ *starts to pace.*] Excuse me, but I haven't been feeling too well lately. I think it's my head. I got hit pretty many times in the head. Did they tell you that?

LEWIS: No.

CZOLGOSZ: Well, it's true. Look . . . [*points to bruises*] . . . they did all that. But it's nothing. [*Pause*] I appreciate your coming here, I really do. It means a great deal to me. You ever spent a night in jail?

LEWIS: I've visited quite a few, but no, never spent the night.

CZOLGOSZ: Neither did I, before this, never in my whole life. I can't sleep in here, not for more than a couple of hours straight. The air just sits where it is, cold and still and stale. [*Pause*] There's nothing you can do for me, but I appreciate your coming here. You must be a fine man. You work for Clarence Darrow?

LEWIS: Mr. Czolgosz, I was appointed by the court this morning to serve as your counsel.

CZOLGOSZ: Oh.

LEWIS: Along with Robert Titus, who couldn't be here today. I've come to ascertain how you would like to plead in this case and to discuss any legal questions you might have. We must enter a plea by tomorrow morning at nine.

CZOLGOSZ: You were appointed.

LEWIS: That is correct. Your refusal to name a counsel of your own left Justice White no choice but to secure a counsel for you. He asked the State Bar Association to recommend someone. The Bar Association provided Justice White with a list of local attorneys, and from that list he chose Mr. Titus and myself. [*Pause*] I feel it is my duty, now, at the outset, to inform you that I have absolutely no sympathy for the creed you espouse –

CZOLGOSZ: The creed?

LEWIS: Allow me to finish, please. [*Pause*] I was disgusted, as all decent Americans were, by your cowardly attack on the President. I have agreed to serve as your counsel because I was requested to do so and, more importantly, because my entire career has been spent upholding the principle of due process. The beauty of our American system of government lies in the fact that even the very lowest criminal rates a fair trial. I might add that Mr. Titus feels the same way. [*Pause*] How do you intend to plead?

CZOLGOSZ: I don't intend to.

LEWIS: Young man, we must enter a plea tomorrow morning.

CZOLGOSZ: You can enter whatever you like, but what you do's got nothing to do with me.

LEWIS: You will have to plead something tomorrow, one way or another.

CZOLGOSZ: I'm not pleading anything tomorrow, or the next day, or the day after that. I don't plead anymore. I used to, every night, used to beg the Lord for all sorts of things. But that didn't work, I found out, it was a waste of time. So I quit pleading, just got up off my knees.

LEWIS: That attitude is not going to change anything The trial will take place, as scheduled, whatever role you decide to play in it.

CZOLGOSZ: I want no part of it.

LEWIS: Then I guess I'll have to enter a plea of Not Guilty on your behalf.

CZOLGOSZ: Not Guilty!

LEWIS: That is the only appropriate plea.

CZOLGOSZ: Let me set you straight. Maybe you haven't seen a newspaper lately. I decided to kill the President, oh, a while ago. So I went out and bought a gun. And the first good chance I got, I pointed the thing at him, pulled the trigger once, pulled it again, hit him with two bullets and now he's dead. [*Pause*]. The only judge I respect holds court right here . . . [*taps himself on head*] . . . and he says I'm guilty. Guilty as hell.

LEWIS: I'm afraid that in New York State the law forbids a defendant accused of First Degree Murder, as you are, from pleading Guilty.

CZOLGOSZ: Is that so.

LEWIS: That is the law.

CZOLGOSZ: Well, it makes sense to me, that your law would have everything, every single thing, ass-backwards – that even though I killed a man in cold blood, in front of thousands of other people, I've got to say in court that I didn't do it, I'm Not Guilty, on account of your law.

LEWIS [*patiently*]: I did not personally draft the law, Mr. Czolgosz, it is the law of this state. I am only trying to inform you of its existence. [*Pause*] We might also plead Not Guilty by Virtue of Insanity.

CZOLGOSZ: You can go plead whatever you like, but that's your plea, not mine. You don't represent me, that court has got no right to judge me, and that little law of yours, well, it's perfect, a perfect sign of the times. Every one of us is guilty of murder, of murder committed under our flag in our name. But now it's against the law to say so, to make a confession. Nobody's allowed to plead Guilty, how about that.

LEWIS: You're getting a little carried away, young man. They warned me you might. This law applies to only one offense: First Degree Murder in New York State. And it's a fine law, an excellent law, especially for someone who doesn't like the government, because it insists that before the state can administer the death penalty, before we can take a man's life, we have to make sure everyone gets to hear the reasons why.

[*Pause*]

CZOLGOSZ [*calmly*]: What I'm saying is, I don't care about the law. It's got nothing to do with me. Maybe that's hard for a lawyer to understand, but that's how I feel. There's your law out there, and there's my law inside of me, and my law's the only one that counts, the only one that matters to me.

LEWIS: And look where that attitude has landed you.

CZOLGOSZ: Murder is murder, Mr. Lewis, sir. Doesn't matter whether you do it yourself, or hire somebody else to do it for you, give him the right uniform and a gun. It's all the same thing.

LEWIS: Are there any witnesses you'd like to call in your behalf? Someone to vouch for your good intentions? I doubt I can find an alienist willing to declare you insane, unless you're willing to ham things up a bit, start frothing at the mouth, walking on all fours, barking. [*Pause*] No? I didn't think so. Insanity is out, then, as our defense. So we'll just enter a plea of Not Guilty and leave it at that.

CZOLGOSZ: Oh, will we?

LEWIS: Unless you'd care to help me put together a defense?

CZOLGOSZ: And if we lose, you going to hang with me?

LEWIS: I certainly hope not, though a lot of people might want me to hang for acting in your defense.

CZOLGOSZ: Woe unto ye lawyers, for ye lade men with grievous burdens, yet ye touch not the burdens with even one of your fingers.

LEWIS: I guess there's nothing further to discuss.

CZOLGOSZ: Jesus didn't like lawyers. You better repent before it's too late.

LEWIS [*stands*]: I'm sorry I couldn't have been of more assistance.

CZOLGOSZ: Don't you get tired, sometimes, of always saying what someone else wants you to say, whether it's right or wrong, the truth or just a bunch of lies? Never speaking for yourself?

LEWIS: It's been a pleasure, Mr. Czolgosz.

CZOLGOSZ: Doing whatever your client wants you to do, like some two-bit hooker –

LEWIS: Washburn –

CZOLGOSZ: You're what's wrong with this country, men like you. Men who're raised since birth, and trained in school, and paid lots of money to never think for themselves, to do whatever they're told by whoever's boss. Living like whores and greasing the machinery that grinds ordinary men down.

[*Pause. They stand face-to-face.* LEWIS *is scared.*]

LEWIS [*louder*]: Washburn –

CZOLGOSZ: Aw, I'd never hurt a lawyer. I could wind up in court.

[*Blackout*]

Scene Three

[ROOSEVELT *sits behind his desk in the Oval Office; across from him sits* MARK HANNA. *On the wall behind them is a huge map of the world, conspicuously dominated by the British Empire, whose territory is everywhere colored bright red.*]

HANNA: And I would like to say, from the bottom of my heart, that if there is a glimmer of light in all this darkness, Teddy, it shines from you.

ROOSEVELT: Why, thank you.

HANNA: It is a blessing that you were Vice President when tragedy struck, a true blessing.

ROOSEVELT: I'll be needing help, a great deal of help, in the coming weeks and months, to shoulder this enormous responsibility on behalf of our fellow Americans.

[*Enter* BROOKS ADAMS, *a slight, bespectacled man, who pauses a few feet away, not wanting to interrupt.*]

HANNA: If there's anything I can do, Mr. President, anything at all, it would be my great honor to be of some service –

ROOSEVELT: Brooks!

ADAMS: Don't let me interrupt –

ROOSEVELT: Nonsense, we were just finishing here. Have you two met?

ADAMS: I don't believe so.

ROOSEVELT: Senator Hanna, I'd like you to meet Brooks Adams, the eminent economist and historian.

[*They shake hands.*]

HANNA: I was seated next to your brother Henry at a dinner once. Very entertaining fellow. Full of opinions. [*Pause*] I'm grateful for this opportunity to meet with you, Mr. President.

ROOSEVELT: We must do this often.

HANNA: I'd be honored. Nice meeting you, Mr. Adams.

ADAMS: A pleasure.

[*Exit* HANNA]

ROOSEVELT: The poor bastard.

ADAMS: He looks much smaller than I'd imagined.

ROOSEVELT: I've been watching him shrink. This hit him harder than anyone except Ida McKinley.

ADAMS: It's hit everyone hard. This whole thing is too extraordinary for words.

ROOSEVELT: Gangrene, that's what they're saying now.

ADAMS: Gangrene?

ROOSEVELT: If I had my way, those doctors would be on trial right beside that filthy anarchist.

ADAMS: I hadn't heard it was gangrene. That's inexcusable.

ROOSEVELT: Brooks, if I ever get shot, just get me some whiskey and a pen knife and I'll do the job myself. I'd trust you with a blade before I'd trust some half-wit gynecologist.

ADAMS: There shouldn't have been a trace of gangrene.

ROOSEVELT: The President was a good and decent man and he deserved better.

[*Pause*]

ADAMS: I see you here, in this office, but I can hardly believe my eyes. Just three weeks ago –

ROOSEVELT: I was about to begin my law studies.

ADAMS: What?

ROOSEVELT: That's right. [*Pause*] With the aid of Judge Parker, I was very quietly going to pursue a law degree while serving as Vice President, in the hope of being admitted to the New York Bar at the end of my term.

ADAMS: Oh, Parker would have loved to see you stuck in the back office of some Wall Street firm.

ROOSEVELT: He suggested Evarts and Choate.

ADAMS: You wouldn't have lasted a week. [*Pause*] How extraordinary.

ROOSEVELT: Now, Brooks, I'm delighted to see you, as always,
but if you're interested in a position, I'm afraid there's
nothing I can do for you at the moment.

ADAMS: That's not –

ROOSEVELT: I've let it be known that business must continue as
usual and that all the President's men will remain in their
posts until things have settled down. Perhaps next year –

ADAMS: I did not come here seeking a position.

ROOSEVELT: Oh.

ADAMS: Though I'm flattered you'd even consider me for one.
[*Pause*] I've come to discuss a matter of far greater import-
ance to us both . . . and to the future of our nation.

ROOSEVELT: I see.

[*Pause*]

ADAMS: You know that I'm hardly a man of superstition.

ROOSEVELT: There's not a mystical bone in your body.

ADAMS: And I've always argued that disorder guides the events
around us. That most things happen for no reason at all.
[*Pause*] Yet I believe some Divine Purpose has placed you
in this office at this time.

ROOSEVELT: Ha!

ADAMS: I mean that, Teddy. I really do. There are rare instances
when the actions of a single man can change everything.
You are that man. And this was no accident.

ROOSEVELT: Brooks, really –

ADAMS: Listen to what I have to say. I know you're busy, terribly
busy, but there are things you must hear now, at the beginning of your Presidency. [*Pause. Then ominously*] The destiny of the United States is in your hands.

[*Pause*]

ROOSEVELT: Well, go ahead then.

61

ADAMS [*almost a whisper*]: According to my calculations, at this moment, as we speak, the seat of international exchanges – the very center of the world economic system – is in motion. [*Pause*] That means we are embarking upon a period of rapidly increasing global turmoil and catastrophe. Those who herald the Twentieth Century as an Age of Peace have not an inkling of what's in store.

ROOSEVELT: You see catastrophe on the horizon?

ADAMS: Oh yes, and plenty of it! The signs are everywhere. When the Bank of England began importing gold to finance their war in South Africa, I knew for certain that the British Empire had begun to fall, and London's days were numbered as the banking capital of the world.

ROOSEVELT: All that gold in Johannesburg, and they have to borrow some from us.

ADAMS: The seat of international exchanges is now in motion, Teddy. And with it goes the most dazzling prize for which any nation can contend: the seat of empire. [*Pause*] From the dawn of Civilization, wherever the seat of exchanges has traveled, it has always brought tremendous power . . . and left disaster in its wake. Along its path, great cities have been built, new religions have been preached, countless rulers have been deified and feared – then all is lost, turned to dust and ruin, as the Law of Civilization and Decay mercilessly dictates the fate of nations.

ROOSEVELT: It's an inescapable law: survival of the fittest.

ADAMS: Survival of the cheapest is more to the point. And the cheaper the better. [*Pause*] That was the Law five thousand years ago, it guided the rise and fall of Babylon and Ninevah, Chaldea and Assyria, Carthage and Phoenicia and any other empire you can name. And that is still the Law today. [*Pause*] Sometimes the seat of exchanges drifts slowly to a new location. Sometimes it moves suddenly, without warning, and with catastrophic effects. The discovery of a new trade route can do it. A string of bad harvests. A pointless war.

ROOSEVELT: Are you certain the seat of exchanges is once again
. . . moving?

ADAMS: Oh, absolutely. I have no doubt that at this very minute
the vortex of the cyclone is approaching New York City.
Already we pour more steel than England, we mine more
coal, they grow lazy and dissolute, and now we see in South
Africa that the British have forgotten how to fight.

ROOSEVELT: Try to buy a pair of riding boots on Bond Street,
and you'll see how the British have lost it, lost the ability to
sell. The salespeople are rude and arrogant and think it's
your great privilege to purchase from them.

ADAMS: The world sees their big navy and their empire and stands
in awe. No one seems to notice the rot spreading from deep
within. The British Empire is finished, and the question then
becomes: what next?

ROOSEVELT: New York.

ADAMS: Yes, yes, all signs point clearly to us. But our supremacy
is by no means a sure thing. The seat of empire might well
leap over New York and land in Tokyo. The Japanese are
a remarkable race, efficient and resourceful. They have
already achieved in two decades what took Englishmen two
centuries to get done.

ROOSEVELT: Clever little bastards, aren't they?

ADAMS: For now, they do not pose much threat. But some day
they might. If we want the great prize, we must seize it and
hold on to it. [*Pause. Then quickly with passion*] Teddy,
you must take up the sword.

ROOSEVELT: Really, Brooks –

ADAMS: You have been thrown into this office by tragedy, yes,
but for a purpose. Now take up the sword! Rockefeller and
Morgan have become our Pompey and Crassus. What the
nation needs now is a Caesar.

ROOSEVELT [*amused*]: But I'm a good Republican.

ADAMS: Listen to what I have to say: The republic we both
loved is dead and buried, gone forever – and it was good

Republicans who killed it. The farmers and frontiersmen have given way, the men of finance have made America their machine, and there is nothing to be done about that, absolutely nothing. These financiers are not our sort. They are Philistines. They never read a book, and their taste is appalling. They love money far more than they love their country. But they are now our masters and we must make sure their machine runs well. [*Pause*] Besides being energetic and industrious, America must be well armed, well organized, and bold. That is the task of the next fifty years, the task that you have been put into this office to begin.

[*Pause*]

ROOSEVELT: I couldn't agree with you more.

ADAMS [*relieved*]: Thank God.

ROOSEVELT: Wouldn't disagree with a word of it.

ADAMS: Teddy, our Army recently went into battle without a general staff, the Treasury struggles every day without proper banking facilities. And our State Department –

ROOSEVELT: It's a disgrace.

ADAMS: Why, the Navy had to scan foreign newspapers to learn the whereabouts of the Spanish fleet.

ROOSEVELT: That won't happen again.

ADAMS: You must make sure. Building the proper administrative structure for empire, that is the task before us. We will need new institutions, a whole new set of attitudes to uphold them, and – more battleships. We will need quite a few more of those.

ROOSEVELT: Of course.

ADAMS: Our future will be measured in battleships.

ROOSEVELT: The changes can't come all at once.

ADAMS: Heavens, no. This will take years, many years, it must. People can't change overnight, they must slowly adapt and with each generation move closer to the ideal. Not every tradition must go. Rome kept its Senate, long after that body ceased to exert any real power. I see no reason why we can't keep ours. [*Pause*] And if all this is done, and done well, and if the movement of the next fifty years only equals that of the last . . . the United States will grow to outweigh any single empire, if not all empires combined. Commerce will flow to us from both the east and the west, and the whole world will bow down to New York and pay tribute.

ROOSEVELT: The Brits are finished – that's for sure.

ADAMS: Now it's up to you.

ROOSEVELT: Don't worry, Brooks.

ADAMS: Some men will oppose you. They will shrink from the great risks involved, tremble at the dangers that lie ahead. What will you say to them?

ROOSEVELT: Out of my way, little tykes.

ADAMS: What about the Founding Fathers, they'll squawk. What about our hallowed traditions? Who needs this empire?

ROOSEVELT: You do, my timid friends. This is your nation and you'll share in its glory or humiliation, whichever may come. Have you heard of Etruria?

ADAMS: That's right –

ROOSEVELT: What do you know of the Aedui, the Ilyrii, the Visigoths, the Celts? Nothing, I'm sure, because those ancient tribes failed.

ADAMS: Vanished –

ROOSEVELT: But you have heard of Rome, no doubt, and even if you haven't, you still live under its sway. Our language, our law, our literature, our system of government, our whole way of looking at life are stamped deep with the imprint of the Romans, because they had the will to prevail.

ADAMS: That's right –

ROOSEVELT: The man who is afraid and risks nothing dies just as surely as the man who risks all to do great things. So, if you're worth a damn, you'll fight for your country with every ounce of your strength, you'll give up your life for it, if need be. And there will come a day, not too far off, perhaps, when you will have to search long and hard for a spot on this earth untouched and unchanged by the mighty spirit of America.

[*Blackout*]

Scene Four

[CZOLGOSZ *sits alone in his cell. After a moment,* WASH-BURN *arrives, pauses, then leans over him.*]

WASHBURN: You didn't say much in court today, Leon.

CZOLGOSZ: Nope.

WASHBURN: Cat got your tongue? [*Pause*] You're not making a very favorable impression on the jury.

[*Pause*]

CZOLGOSZ: Maybe you'd like to take the stand.

WASHBURN: Oh boy –

CZOLGOSZ: Say a few words in my defense: A true gentleman. A fine man. A true patriot. In our brief time together, our enforced companionship, I've come to love him like a brother.

WASHBURN: You don't want me on the stand. The judge'd bang the trial to a close right afterward, and they'd drag you out of court kicking and screaming.

CZOLGOSZ: Just leave me alone.

[*Pause*]

WASHBURN: What is it with you?

CZOLGOSZ: Huh?

WASHBURN: I said, what is it with you?

CZOLGOSZ: Washburn, I'm tired.

WASHBURN: Seems all you can do is insult people and complain about things.

CZOLGOSZ: Let me have some peace.

WASHBURN: Everybody I know's been asking me about you. Everybody's curious. My wife asks me, what kind of voice does he have? Is it real low and spooky, does he sound like a monster?

CZOLGOSZ: Your wife asked that, you've got a wife?

WASHBURN: That's right.

CZOLGOSZ: Well, bring her over here. I'd like a look at Washburn's wife.

WASHBURN: She's pretty as can be.

CZOLGOSZ: She marry you for the money, then? Or is she blind?

WASHBURN: She married me for me.

CZOLGOSZ: So she's deaf, dumb and blind?

WASHBURN: Take it easy, there.

CZOLGOSZ: Bring her over here. She sounds like fun.

[*Pause*]

WASHBURN: We're looking to buy a farm.

CZOLGOSZ [*sincere*]: Is that so?

WASHBURN: My father's got a farm, over a hundred acres, but my brother gets it.

CZOLGOSZ: Older brother?

WASHBURN: Eleven months older.

CZOLGOSZ: Nature's unkind.

WASHBURN: That's why I'm working here for the time being. We want pigs, chickens, cows, the whole thing.

CZOLGOSZ: A couple of dogs.

WASHBURN: That's right.

[*Pause*]

CZOLGOSZ: Farms come pretty cheap these days, don't they?

WASHBURN: Not cheap enough.

CZOLGOSZ: Well there's farmers going broke left and right.

WASHBURN: No there ain't, not around here.

CZOLGOSZ: It's happening all around the country, Washburn, the best farmers, the best land, getting foreclosed.

WASHBURN: My pa's doing fine.

CZOLGOSZ: I'm not making this up.

WASHBURN: I know this entire area and things are fine.

CZOLGOSZ: If crop prices fall any lower, some farmer will pay you to take the land off his hands, give you the great privilege of keeping bankers rich and fat and lazy.

WASHBURN: What is it with you? [*Pause*] What makes you need to insult everybody, knock everything down? That's what I want to know.

CZOLGOSZ: It's none of your business.

WASHBURN: Most people, Leon, they try real hard to learn what they're supposed to do. And then they spend their whole life trying to do it – just trying to do what they're supposed to do, with no fanfare.

CZOLGOSZ: That describes me, too.

WASHBURN: Oh, not a chance.

CZOLGOSZ: That's what I've done.

WASHBURN: Most people don't throw away their lives, for nothing. They don't kill innocent people and then act boastful and vain and arrogant about it.

CZOLGOSZ: Oh, yes they do. With flags waving.

WASHBURN: There's no use talking to you.

CZOLGOSZ: Glad you figured that out.

[*Pause*]

WASHBURN: Getting a little scared?

CZOLGOSZ: Not yet.

WASHBURN: It ain't going to be pleasant.

CZOLGOSZ: Couldn't be worse than this.

WASHBURN: If there's a Hell, Leon, you're going to get real acquainted with it.

[*Blackout*]

Scene Five

[ROOSEVELT, *wearing silk pajamas and a dressing gown, slowly paces back and forth, barefoot. His wife,* EDITH, *sleeps nearby in bed. The stage is dimly lit.* ROOSEVELT *stops, glances at* EDITH *for a moment, then starts pacing again. She lifts her head, sees him awake, and rises from bed.* EDITH *is tall, elegant, and aristocratic. Her long white nightgown seems proper and Victorian, yet vaguely transparent. The President and the First Lady are a young, attractive couple.*]

EDITH: Darling, what is it?

ROOSEVELT: I must write to him.

EDITH: To whom?

ROOSEVELT: Peabody.

EDITH: Oh, darling, I thought you'd decided not to.

ROOSEVELT: My mind keeps wandering toward the matter, when I really ought to be concentrating on other things.

EDITH: Then you should write him, straight away.

ROOSEVELT: You think so?

EDITH: Let him know you're concerned.

ROOSEVELT: Should I?

EDITH: Share your thoughts with him.

ROOSEVELT: It would have to be kept strictly confidential.

EDITH: Mr. Peabody can be trusted.

ROOSEVELT: If Teddy ever thought I was trying to interfere –

EDITH: You have a right to be concerned about your son and a right to share your thoughts.

[*Pause*]

ROOSEVELT [*angry*]: I just don't think it's worth the risk. If Teddy gets too battered up now, it could affect his chances of playing on the class team when he gets to Harvard.

EDITH: Darling, he's only fourteen. Now come to bed.

ROOSEVELT: I spoke to De Saulles, the Yale quarterback, about it, and he said that a young boy shouldn't get too battered up playing against bigger boys. It might interfere with his playing later.

EDITH: Perhaps you should have him talk to Teddy.

ROOSEVELT [*angrier*]: De Saulles? I don't want De Saulles talking to him.

EDITH: Sweetheart, come to bed.

ROOSEVELT: If anyone tells Teddy, it should be me.

[*Pause*]

EDITH: I don't think it's a bad idea to ask Mr. Peabody's advice. He sees boys come and go at Groton, with minor scrapes and bloody noses every year.

ROOSEVELT: That tooth will be black for the rest of his life.

EDITH: Darling, I'm not encouraging him to play football.

ROOSEVELT: I don't want him to feel any bitterness towards me. I don't want him to feel he missed his chance or fell in popularity among his school chums on my account. [*Pause*] But he's just not big enough.

EDITH: You can write Mr. Peabody tomorrow. Teddy need never know.

ROOSEVELT: Football is a rough and manly sport, and I'm glad he likes it. I am glad that he boxes and rows and rides and shoots as well as he does, with such fine spirit. But I don't want him to devote too much of his energies, or even the major portion of his energies, to these things, without the proper sense.

EDITH: And neither do I.

ROOSEVELT: He should develop his physical prowess up to a certain point, but after he has reached that point, there are other things that count more.

EDITH: Many other things.

ROOSEVELT: Edith, in my regiment, nine-tenths of the men were better horsemen than I was and two-thirds were better with a rifle. Yet after I had them a very short while, they all knew, and I knew too, that nobody else could command them as I could.

EDITH: Have you told that to Teddy?

ROOSEVELT: Of course I have.

[*Pause*]

EDITH: Come along.

[*She takes* ROOSEVELT *by the hand and gently leads him back to bed.* EDITH *gets under the covers.* ROOSEVELT *takes off his dressing gown, then sits on the edge of the bed.*]

ROOSEVELT: Think about their house in Canton – the living room.

EDITH: I know.

ROOSEVELT: That quilt that Ida made, above the couch.

EDITH: She spent months on it.

ROOSEVELT: He was President of the United States and lived in that house. You'd think it belonged to a division superintendent of the New York Central Railway.

EDITH: She never wanted to leave it.

ROOSEVELT: He wasn't even a man of moderate means. He wore the same damn suit, day after day. [*Pause*] I have seen enough of human nature not to be astounded at ordinary folly or ordinary wickedness. But I can hardly believe, at this time, in this country, that any human being could be so infamous a scoundrel, so crazy a fool, as to assassinate this President. And somehow consider his murder an assault upon wealth and privilege. [*Pause*] It is incredible. It is incomprehensible.

[EDITH *leans forward, drapes an arm across his chest, and rests her chin on his shoulder.*]

EDITH [*softly*]: Come to bed.

[*Blackout*]

Scene Six

[LEWIS *stands center-stage, addressing the audience as though it were judge and jury.*]

LEWIS: If your Honor please, the defendant has no witnesses that he will call and refuses to testify on his own behalf, so that testimony is closed at the close of the testimony of the People. [*Pause*] I must admit that my colleague and I are somewhat embarrassed by the testimony closing at this point. But we have had little time to consult with one another and have received no help whatsoever from the defendant. [*Pause*] You sat here and heard for yourselves that the defendant pleaded Guilty when he was arraigned by the District Attorney. But the law of our state will not permit such a plea in a crime like this, and you must ignore the defendant's impertinent remarks and base your verdict solely on the evidence introduced in this courtroom. [*Long pause*] I believe it has been demonstrated, beyond any peradventure of doubt, that the President was stricken down at the hand of the defendant. What you must now decide is how he should be punished for committing this crime. Please keep in mind that every human being has a powerful desire to live. Death is a specter that none of us would like to encounter soon. And before you conjure that specter for this young man, think long and hard about the highly unusual facts of this case. [*Pause*] I would like to close the defense with a few words of a personal nature. [*Pause*] I believe William McKinley was the noblest man that God ever created on the soil of the United States. A man of irreproachable character. A loving husband, a good man in every aspect that you could conceive of. And his death, his brutal, senseless murder, has been the saddest blow to me in many, many years. [*Pause*] The time has come to vindicate the rule of law in this country and to make a certain class of people feel the strong arm of justice before another calamity can strike again. [*Pause*] The defense rests its case.

[*Blackout*]

Scene Seven

[ROOSEVELT *sits behind his desk in the Oval Office. Across from him sit* A. T. MAHAN, *a short, elderly man in a U.S. Navy uniform, and* SPECK VON STERNBURG, *who is younger, very polished, and very German.*]

ROOSEVELT: The *Oregon* is what, nine thousand tons?

MAHAN: Eight or nine.

ROOSEVELT: Say nine thousand.

STERNBURG: Soon they will be built *twice* that size.

MAHAN: Nonsense.

STERNBURG: Within five years. These battleships will be the most awesome weapons of destruction that mankind has ever invented. One of them could hold its own, most likely could prevail, against the entire U.S. battle fleet of 1898. Just one of them.

ROOSEVELT: Admiral, could such a ship ever be built?

[*Pause*]

MAHAN: I have long believed that what we urgently need is not a bigger battleship, but an agreement among naval officers the world over on the size of a standard battleship, a standard that all navies will promise to abide by, so that victory is the just reward for superior strategy, not tonnage.

STERNBURG: That is my idea of nonsense.

ROOSEVELT: I asked whether such giant battleships could ever be built.

MAHAN: Perhaps. [*Pause*] I think we could probably build a

twenty-thousand-ton ship right now, if we cared to do so.
But I don't think we should, it would be much too slow.
And there are other considerations.

ROOSEVELT: Such as?

MAHAN: Considerations we might discuss another time.

ROOSEVELT: Mr. von Sternburg is a private citizen, not a representative of the German government, and he is a friend of mine.

MAHAN: There are . . . political considerations. The introduction of larger ships, if indeed they should prove superior, will render the existing ships in every fleet obsolete. These will all have to be replaced by the newer size, until that size becomes obsolete, and on and on, as ships remain useful for only a few years and then must be scrapped. Why persist in adding ton after ton, like a drunkard running up a bill at the bar? [*Pause*] If we want a big navy, Mr. President, it must be composed of reasonably sized ships. Congress is sure to balk as battleships grow bigger and naturally more expensive. [*To* STERNBURG] We are hampered here by democracy in ways that your army and navy are not.

ROOSEVELT: In this agreement, would you only place limits on size?

MAHAN: We could start by limiting the size, by achieving an international consensus on a standard battleship.

STERNBURG: That will never happen.

MAHAN: And from there we could go on to reach agreement on the number of battleships each navy may build.

STERNBURG: Limit the number of ships? Based on what? The balance of power last week, last year, or in the days of William the Conqueror?

MAHAN: An agreed-upon formula.

STERNBURG: At the moment, the Royal Navy is maintained at a numerical strength equal to the combined navies of any other two nations in the world. That is the British formula. Would you force them to abandon it?

MAHAN: I don't think the Royal Navy poses much of a threat to us.

STERNBURG: Mr. President, are these shiny new battleships of yours meant to serve as a mere coast guard? Are you saying the United States and Germany must acquiesce forever to British control of the seas?

ROOSEVELT: Well, I –

[A MESSENGER *arrives.*]

ROOSEVELT: One minute.

MAHAN: Mr. von Sternburg, I'm afraid you will find a growing desire among Americans for a closer relationship with England.

STERNBURG: Oh, that is not my perception. I think it is safe to say, on the basis of reading your newspapers, that there is no nation on earth that Americans hate more than England.

MAHAN: Perhaps you read too many Democratic newspapers.

STERNBURG: If Russia were to invade India tomorrow, as she very well may, or seize Afghanistan, the American people would applaud Russia's courage.

MAHAN: I'm a little lost in this conversation.

STERNBURG: You cannot deny that the American people would root for Russia in any war against the British.

MAHAN: We seem to have gone from imaginary battleships to imaginary wars.

ROOSEVELT: Gentlemen, please. There's no disputing the fact that of all the nations in Europe, Americans like Russia the most.

STERNBURG: Don't let your navy become a tool of the British Empire. The British are very clever, and they want to use you, that's all.

ROOSEVELT [*calmly*]: Now, listen here. We are building a great navy to defend American interests, not British interests, not German interests, not Chinese or Peruvian interests – American interests.

STERNBURG: I didn't mean to imply –

ROOSEVELT [*firmly*]: I'm sure you didn't. [*Pause*] Now, Admiral, you are correct about one thing. In this country there is indeed some opposition to building a first-class fleet of battleships. Much of the squawking comes from over-educated types, from the sort who believes in peace at any price. Some of these men are well-intended. They think the United States can be protected by treaties. They honestly believe it, despite the fact that every war begins with the breaking of a treaty. In the absence of a strong navy, treaties are just pieces of paper. You can tear them apart [*lifting a memo from his desk, then ripping it*], like that. Some of my opponents, however, are not merely naïve. They are beneath contempt. They are men in name only – socialists, anarchist sympathizers, soft-headed disciples of Tolstoy. Their prattle about the love of mankind has become a substitute for loving their own country. I want peace as much as any man. More, even, than the cowards who've never set foot on a battlefield. I've seen war, I've been in the thick of it. On Kettle hill my young orderly stood to salute me, took a bullet through the throat, and fell dead right across my knees. I looked right at the face of a young Spanish soldier, then shot and killed him with my revolver. The gun was a gift from my brother-in-law, and it had been recovered from the sunken battleship *Maine*. That young Spaniard paid dearly for his country's insolent attack upon mine. [*Pause*] Gentlemen, I have seen war. And I am convinced that preparation for war is the best guarantee of peace.

STERNBURG [*trying to please*]: That's what George Washington thought.

ROOSEVELT: That is what most Americans think. We will build as many battleships as we need, and we'll build them as large as we like. Congress will see to it, don't you doubt that. We don't acknowledge any limits, in whatever we do, and we're not about to start while I'm in charge. That's one lesson the world had better learn.

[*Pause. Then* ROOSEVELT *notices the* MESSENGER, *who has been standing aside, discreet and forgotten.*]

ROOSEVELT: Yes?

MESSENGER: A telegram from Buffalo, sir.

ROOSEVELT: Well, read the damn thing.

MESSENGER [*reads*]: "After twenty-seven minutes of deliberation the jury has found the defendant Guilty of Murder in the First Degree."

ROOSEVELT: What about the sentence?

MESSENGER [*reads*]: "The sentence of the court is as follows: that in the week beginning on October 28, 1901, at the place, in the manner, and by the means prescribed by law, Leon Czolgosz must suffer the penalty of death."

STERNBURG: Bully!

MAHAN: Well, that's splendid.

ROOSEVELT: Thank you, son. [*Exit* MESSENGER] Now where were we?

[*Blackout*]

Scene Eight

[CZOLGOSZ *and* BULL *sit on stools in the prison cell, late at night.*]

CZOLGOSZ: Whenever I pissed it hurt like hell.

BULL: Jesus.

CZOLGOSZ: Felt like burning kerosene.

BULL: Ow.

CZOLGOSZ: That's how I found out. Nice way to find out.

BULL: What did you say to her?

CZOLGOSZ: Nothing. [*Pause*] Never said a word. We were

77

supposed to meet that Friday at some coffee house, bu[t]
chose not to show up. Never saw her again. Never sa[w]
another word.

BULL: That's rough.

[*Long pause*]

CZOLGOSZ: She was a socialist and that sort of put me o[ff]
socialism.

BULL: I bet.

CZOLGOSZ: You can't hold everything in common. Some thin[gs]
were never meant to be held in common. I learned that t[he]
hard way, it was a painful lesson. [BULL *laughs*] To h[ell]
with Karl Marx.

BULL: Your father thought you'd never had a girlfriend.

CZOLGOSZ: He hasn't known about me since I was ten years o[ld].

BULL: What was the name of this socialist gal?

CZOLGOSZ: Oh, no. No need for that.

[*Pause.* BULL *removes a flask from his jacket pocket a[nd]
offers it to* CZOLGOSZ, *who declines.*]

BULL: Sure?

CZOLGOSZ: Haven't had a drop in three years. Hate to start no[w].

BULL: Mind if I?

CZOLGOSZ: Nope. [BULL *takes a swig. Pause*] What're you doi[ng]
here, anyway? Is this a practice of yours?

BULL: Yes, it is.

[*Pause*]

CZOLGOSZ: You're not just snooping around, huh? Fishing.

BULL: No, I'm not. I'm interested.

CZOLGOSZ: You're interested.

BULL: That's all.

CZOLGOSZ: I'd like to believe it.

[*Silence*]

ULL: You said you were sick when you quit that job?

ZOLGOSZ: Yeah, I was sick. [*Pause*] Sick of everything around me.

ULL: I mean from the gal, how bad did it get?

ZOLGOSZ: Oh, I got over that business in a month or two. The problem just went away on its own, the physical aspect. But after that, I'd had enough. [*Pause*] I could see everything crystal clear, whether I wanted to or not, it was right there. [*Pause*] Ever crack one of your teeth?

ULL: Don't think I have.

ZOLGOSZ: Believe me, you'd remember.

ULL: My wife has.

ZOLGOSZ: The nerves inside your teeth, Christ, are they sharp. Most of the time, you don't think much about them, because they're covered over – until some tooth gets its outer part broken away. Then it's a whole new mouth. You breathe the wrong way, my friend, and it hurts like hell, living hell.

ULL: What happened, you chipped some teeth?

ZOLGOSZ: No, I didn't, that's not what I'm talking about. I'm trying to explain how I felt and all I can think about is broken teeth. [*Pause*] I'd thought about things before, thought I had it all figured out, but thinking something and feeling it are worlds apart. I mean feeling it so hard you don't know what to do. There's this tight knot in your gut and another in your throat and you don't know whether to lie down, or go outside, or get a drink of something, or start crying. [*Pause*] That's how I felt, for months. I would lie in bed at night praying the feeling would go away, but I'd wake up the next day with it and wish I didn't have to get out of bed. Walking down the street, I'd look over at people and somehow, I'd be feeling what they were feeling, like I was them. That's not something you want to do, when there are lots of men out of work and sleeping in the street, when there's people in misery all over the place. It's a lot better to just look straight ahead and keep walking without feeling every goddamn thing around you.

BULL: Sounds pretty bad.

CZOLGOSZ: Oh, it was. Got so I couldn't enjoy anything. [*Pause*] Couldn't even look at a newspaper without feeling sick.

BULL: Good for you.

CZOLGOSZ: You don't understand –

BULL: They get me upset, too. All the sensationalism.

CZOLGOSZ: Reading the newspaper –

BULL: They make a big ruckus out of every little crime here.

CZOLGOSZ: Reading the newspaper was always my favorite part of the day.

BULL: Not me.

CZOLGOSZ: I didn't tell the reporter that, but I'm telling you.

BULL: Don't care much for reporters, either.

[*Pause*]

CZOLGOSZ: Every morning, I used to read straight through, from the upper left-hand corner on page one to the lower right-hand corner on the back. I read everything, the whole damn paper. Took me off to all sorts of places, around the world, like I was part of it all. [*Pause*] Then I couldn't look at it anymore. Couldn't bear to. It wasn't just words on paper anymore, it was alive for me, it was life. Concentration camps in South Africa, Filipino villages being torched, on every page a new horror, thoughts I couldn't leave behind when I got to the baseball scores. [*Pause*] It got so I didn't want to be around people anymore, because I could feel the tragedy of their lives. Whether I wanted to or not, I saw the full dimension of it. No matter how much I tried, I couldn't get back my old covering, the solid wall you need to keep you from the truth of things. Without that wall, you can't look at people's faces on the trolley car or read about the famine in India, you can't do it. It's not possible. [*Pause*] That's when I stopped going to the factory.

BULL: Did you talk to anyone about this?

CZOLGOSZ: Not really.

BULL: Wasn't there someone you could talk to?

CZOLGOSZ: I tried talking to the foreman, Jack, he was always good to me because I worked hard. He asked if something was wrong one day, so I told him. Told him some of these things. But he didn't see what I meant, not at all. He just looked at me like I was speaking Chinese, some strange language he'd never heard before.

BULL: What did he say?

CZOLGOSZ: You live on earth, Leon, and there's no cure for that.

BULL: That's some help.

CZOLGOSZ: That's no help at all. That's worse than no help.

BULL: So that's when you quit.

CZOLGOSZ: I said Jake, it's time for me to retire.

BULL: And what did he say?

CZOLGOSZ: He laughed at me. And I could hear him laughing, over all that noise in the mill, until I was nearly out of the building.

BULL: He didn't try to keep you on?

CZOLGOSZ: Like I said, he just laughed, like it was something real funny. [*Pause*] So I went to live on the farm, our farm way outside of town. [*Pause*] I read a lot of books and stayed away from other people as much as I could.

BULL: What about your family?

CZOLGOSZ: They were around, but I stayed away from them, too.

BULL: How long did you spend there, on the farm?

CZOLGOSZ: Oh, a while.

BULL: Did you take any trips?

CZOLGOSZ: No, I was there a while, steady, over a year. [*Pause*] But still, I couldn't get away from the filth, from the shit of this day and age. There was too much of it in me and it went wherever I did. Couldn't leave it behind someplace, all neat and wrapped up. Something must be done, my mind started telling me, something must be done. Feeding the pigs wasn't the answer and fiddling around in the garden wasn't it either. The world was still out there, beyond the fence post. I saw how things were going and where it all would lead to, and I couldn't pretend that I didn't see. Something must be done, my mind was telling me, something must be done. [*Pause*] One day I got my father's shotgun and started shooting at birds, hunting things like he'd always wanted me to. I'd never shot a gun before –

BULL: Never?

CZOLGOSZ: I'd never killed anything bigger than a fly, but now I needed to learn how, to see what it looked like up close. I needed to hollow myself out, get rid of what was soft, build myself a good thick wall before leaving the farm and doing what I knew I had to do.

[*Long pause*]

BULL: You know, Leon, I voted against McKinley twice. Never liked what he stood for.

CZOLGOSZ: Is that so?

BULL: I liked him, but not what he stood for. I'm against this empire business myself. A lot of people are. We've got enough to worry about in this country. We shouldn't be wasting time and money trying to solve the world's problems.

CZOLGOSZ: Well, well.

BULL: Something's got to be done, all right, but you went about it all wrong. You see that now, don't you?

CZOLGOSZ: It wasn't easy, what I did.

BULL: It was an awful mistake, though. You can admit that now.

CZOLGOSZ: The American people are sleepwalking.

BULL: Now's the time to be honest with yourself.

CZOLGOSZ: Somebody had to yell: "Wake up, you're headed the wrong way."

BULL: You made an awful mistake, Leon. Have the guts to admit it to yourself.

CZOLGOSZ: Maybe it didn't make sense from a . . . practical point of view. But doing what's right isn't always the practical thing to do.

BULL: This man in the White House is about a thousand times worse and you can sit here and say you're not sorry?

CZOLGOSZ: I didn't say I wasn't sorry.

BULL: Then be a man and just say it, say you're sorry you did it.

CZOLGOSZ: I'll say this. I wish one of your boys had killed me right on the spot, right there with the President. I'm sorry that didn't happen. I'm awful sorry about that.

[*Blackout*]

Scene Nine

[IDA MCKINLEY, *dressed in black, sits in a rocking chair. She is knitting a pink babysuit. Beside her, on a table, is a photograph of her late husband in an ornate silver frame. She knits and gently rocks for a few moments.*]

IDA: Mark. [*Pause*] Mark –

HANNA [*from offstage*]: Coming, Ida.

[*Enter* HANNA]

IDA: What time is it now?

HANNA: Quarter to seven.

IDA: He's late.

HANNA: I know.

IDA: He *is* coming?

HANNA: Yes.

IDA: You made sure?

HANNA: Yes I did.

IDA: Well, I wonder where he is.

[*Pause*]

HANNA: Now, Ida, you have to promise me one thing.

IDA: I promise.

HANNA: This is highly unorthodox and word of it must never leak out.

IDA: I promise.

HANNA: I've gone to great trouble making the arrangements and you have to give me your word.

IDA: Oh, I promise, it's our little secret. I promised yesterday and I'll promise again tomorrow, if you like. He *is* coming?

HANNA: Yes.

[IDA *returns to her knitting and* HANNA *paces, hands behind his back, waiting. Long pause. The doorbell rings.*]

IDA: That must be him.

HANNA: I'll go see.

[*Exit* HANNA. IDA *stops, waits.* HANNA *returns with an extremely uncomfortable* PAUL CZOLGOSZ. IDA *sees him, feebly stands, extends her hand.*]

IDA: I'm Ida McKinley.

PAUL: It is an honor to meet you. [*He bows slightly*] My name is Paul Czolgosz. [*Very long, awkward pause*] I cannot tell you how sorry I am about what happened. How sorry I am for you, Mrs. McKinley. I lost a wife many years ago. I cannot say how much I wish this never happened. The President was a great man, very great.

IDA: Yes he was. [*Pause*] Mark, could you bring this gentleman a chair?

PAUL: No, please.

IDA: There's one in the hall.

[*Exit* HANNA. IDA *sits in her rocking chair.* PAUL *stands straight and tall but fidgets with the train ticket in his hand.*]

IDA: You've come a long way?

PAUL: From Cleveland, not too long.

IDA: Would you like a cool drink?

PAUL: No, no, I'm fine. Thank you.

IDA: Have you ever been to Canton before?

PAUL: No, I never have.

IDA: This is where I grew up.

PAUL: It's nice, it looks very nice.

[HANNA *returns with a chair.* PAUL *sits, after a moment's hesitation, while* HANNA *stands behind him. Long pause.*]

IDA: What was your son like . . . as a boy?

PAUL: My son? [*Pause*] He was a good little boy.

IDA: There wasn't something wicked about him . . . from the very start?

PAUL: Oh, no. Not that I could see. I used to think he would become a priest, so serious.

IDA: A Catholic priest?

PAUL: Yes, we are Catholic.

IDA: You say he was a good boy, but what was he like?

PAUL: The problem with my son is that he is weak. He was always weak. He was not like the other boys, he would not play like them. He prefer his mother, he spend too much time with her. If I blame myself at all for him, I blame myself for not taking him away from his mother. She meant well, but she spoiled him.

IDA: Her heart must be broken.

PAUL: No, like I said, she died many years ago. She did not have to see this, thank the Lord. He was her favorite, Leon was always her favorite.

IDA: Was he simply crushed when she passed away?

PAUL: Oh, yes. We were all very upset. But Leon, he stayed upset the longest. [*Pause*] I want you to know, I love my son, but tomorrow he gets what he deserves. The President was a great man, my son had no right to do that.

IDA: Your son is going to be killed tomorrow.

PAUL: I know. But it is the right thing for what he did.

IDA: You are about to lose your son.

PAUL: I have other sons.

[*Pause*]

IDA: How old is this one, your son Leon?

PAUL: Twenty-seven. I think.

IDA: That is young. He is still a young man. Surely you object to his being killed tomorrow.

PAUL: I am sad but it is the right thing.

HANNA: He doesn't object.

IDA: You must object.

HANNA: He doesn't.

IDA: Well, I do. [*Pause*] I do not want this boy to be killed tomorrow.

HANNA: Ida, the court –

IDA: I don't care about the court. I don't care what the court says, I say this young boy should not be killed. This is his father here. I don't see any point.

HANNA: Justice must be served.

IDA: I don't think it's justice, killing a young boy like that. Killing a young boy won't bring my husband back.

HANNA: We are talking about the President's assassin.

IDA: Not *the* President, *my* husband, and he would not want this done, I know it. My husband's spirit is looming above us and it says do not kill the boy. Do not kill the boy for my sake.

HANNA: Ida, please, be calm.

IDA: I will not. My husband was a good Christian and he believed in Christian mercy and he would say to you that killing this boy will not accomplish a thing.

HANNA: It can serve as an example.

IDA: It should serve as an example that the killing must stop. It must stop. Unless the killing stops now it will simply go on and on. When will the killing stop? You tell me when. I am sick of it and I want it to stop. Life is too precious. I demand that the killing stop.

HANNA: Ida, this was more than an assault on your husband. This was an attack upon the basic principles of this country.

IDA: This young boy must not be killed. Mark, I want you to stop it. I want this murder called off.

HANNA: There's nothing I can do.

IDA: Oh yes there is. You can have it called off.

HANNA: I can't overrule a New York State court.

IDA: You can tell them I want it stopped. You can tell them that or I'll tell them.

HANNA: Ida –

IDA: I'll tell them it must be stopped. I will tell the newspapers exactly what I think.

PAUL: Please –

IDA: This is your son. You should fight for his life. He's your son.

HANNA [*to Paul*]: I think you had better go.

IDA: I will tell the newspapers. I am going to demand that this be stopped.

HANNA [*to Paul*]: Please wait in the hall.

IDA: I will not allow another murder to take place. I don't see the point and the newspapers will make sure that my wishes are respected.

HANNA: The President would have wanted the law to be obeyed.

IDA: My husband was a good Christian, a man of mercy. Not just a politician. He was much, much more than that. To you he was a politician, that's how he was useful to you.

HANNA: Charlotte!

IDA: I will not allow this young boy to be murdered. I will not allow it.

HANNA: Charlotte, come downstairs –

[*Blackout*]

Scene Ten

[JONAS *stands at the foot of the stage, addressing the audience.*]

JONAS [*very nervous*]: It's a simple contraption, simple but a real advance, because it's more reliable than before and faster, yes it's much faster. [*Spotlight slowly comes up on an electric chair, behind* JONAS, *mounted atop a small platform center-stage*] Seventeen hundred volts is what it is, sent, uh, directly to the skull through that helmet you see back there. [*Pause*] I wired it myself. We have had more than a dozen . . . we've tried it more than a dozen times and it's worked, it's always done what it's supposed to. [*Pause*] Lately we buckle a leather-backed sponge soaked with salt water behind each knee and put a wet sponge in the helmet to make extra sure the electrical circuit doesn't somehow get broken. [*Pause*] Well, that's about it. Sometimes the contortions can get awful gruesome. I ought to warn you about that. And the aroma, it has an effect on some folks. You might want to keep your handkerchief handy.

[JONAS *stands aside and waits, next to a large switch.* BULL *and* WASHBURN *enter with* CZOLGOSZ.]

BULL: Would you like to see a priest?

CZOLGOSZ: No.

BULL: Are you sure? We can get you a priest.

CZOLGOSZ: I don't want one.

BULL: He's in the building.

CZOLGOSZ: I don't want to see him. [*Pause*] But would you please ask him to say a prayer for my father, say something for his sake?

BULL: I'll do that.

[*They walk center-stage.*]

BULL: Anything you want to say to these people here?

CZOLGOSZ: Yes.

WASHBURN: Keep it brief, Leon.

CZOLGOSZ [*to audience, calmly*]: I would like to say a few words to you. I would like to say this: I killed the President on behalf of all the good people of this country, the good working people. Because this President was a murderer and a tyrant. [*Pause. Then hard and fanatic*] And as for all of you, who came here to watch this: You are going to be punished for what your government is doing right now, or your children will pay the price for your outrageous vanity. And when this great nation of ours goes up in flames, when our cities are in ruins, and there's nothing but rubble and ashes from coast to coast, don't say nobody warned you. Don't say it wasn't your fault. When it comes, you deserve it, and I told you so.

[*Pause*]

WASHBURN: That it?

CZOLGOSZ: That's all from me.

WASHBURN: Let's go, then.

[CZOLGOSZ *is led to the chair and calmly sits in it, staring at the audience as* WASHBURN *and* BULL *bind his wrists and ankles, place the helmet on his head, and, lastly, tie a wide leather strap across his face. It obscures all but his eyes from view.* WASHBURN *and* BULL *step down from the platform.*]

BULL: May God have mercy on your soul. [*Pause*] Go ahead, Jonas.

WASHBURN: Give him a good poke.

[JONAS *pulls the switch and suddenly the stage is brilliantly lit in white light. For the next few seconds, the chair rattles,* CZOLGOSZ *violently shakes, and a tiny wisp of white smoke*

wafts upwards from the helmet. Silence. Then CZOLGOSZ
kicks the chair.]

BULL: Maybe we ought to try again.

[JONAS *pulls the switch again. Blackout. And the curtain
falls.*]

Dramatis Personae

MILBURN, a foreman
MARK HANNA, a political boss
JONAS, an electrician
WILLIAM MCKINLEY, a beloved President
a GUIDE to the exposition
LEON CZOLGOSZ, an anarchist
MATTHEW D. MANN, a gynecologist
WILLIAM BULL, a chief of police
FOSTER of the Secret Service
WASHBURN, a prison guard
IDA MCKINLEY, the First Lady
DORIS, her companion
JOHN NOWAK, a saloon keeper
PAUL CZOLGOSZ, the anarchist's father
ARTHUR HAMILTON, a reporter
CLARK, Hanna's nephew
2 VALETS
the REVEREND
THEODORE ROOSEVELT, the new President
LORAN L. LEWIS, a defense attorney
BROOKS ADAMS, an eccentric historian
EDITH ROOSEVELT, the new First Lady
A. T. MAHAN, an old admiral
SPECK VON STERNBURG, a German aristocrat
a MESSENGER

Afterword

I wrote *Americans* in 1985. I'd spent the previous few years studying British imperial history, trying to comprehend why empires rise and fall. I was particularly interested in the period between 1898 and 1902, when the British Empire began to stumble, America's empire was born, and a "special relationship" between the two nations was secretly formed amid colonial wars in South Africa and the Philippines. The end of the century marked an historic turning-point, a convergence of imperial paths that soon transformed the world. Longstanding attitudes changed, and traditional roles were reversed. At the beginning of the 1890s, Americans still embraced a revolutionary foreign policy: friendship with all nations, entangling alliances with none. The United States was the world's leading industrial power, but did not possess a single battleship and had only 25,000 men in its army. Great Britain was the world's dominant financial and military power. Its banks supplied capital to Wall Street, and its navy maintained eleven bases and thirty-three coaling stations in the seas around the United States, ensuring those loans would be repaid. Although wealthy members of the East Coast establishment admired the British Empire and sought entry to its upper class, most Americans despised both. The hatred of Great Britain was so widespread and intense that William McKinley, running for President in 1896 as Wall Street's candidate, felt it necessary to circulate a pamphlet entitled, "How McKinley is Hated in England".

After writing a graduate thesis that looked at the origins of the

Anglo-American military alliance, I thought about how to address some of the issues in a form that would be more accessible and provocative. How America became the world's mightiest empire did not seem like a purely academic question. Ronald Reagan was president of the United States at the time; Margaret Thatcher was prime minister of England; and many of the old imperial attitudes were being brought down from the attic, dusted off, and given a new spin for a new generation. The late twentieth century reminded me of the late nineteenth in a number of other ways. On both sides of the Atlantic, worship of the "free market", growing corporate power, union-busting and a widening gap between rich and poor suggested the dawn of another Gilded Age.

The story of William McKinley's assassination seemed like a good way to explore these historical parallels. It also seemed like a great story, rich with irony and unintended consequences. Here was Theodore Roosevelt, America's first modern president, a supreme nationalist and imperialist, thrust into office by an anarchist who opposed all state power. A history play, borrowing from Shakespeare and Camus, about the birth of an empire – why not? I was twenty-five years old. I thought the subject was timely and important. Unfortunately, I couldn't find a producer who agreed. I sent the play to countless theater companies in the United States and Great Britain, to companies that were well-known, unknown, fringe, painfully obscure. Aside from a few readings and one or two close calls, none was interested. The play went into my filing cabinet in 1989, where it remained for the next twelve years.

During the first week of September 2001, my wife and I wandered through the forum in Rome, looking at the ruins, discussing what the ruins of our home town, New York City, might look like some day. On September 11 I rode my bicycle down to the World Trade Center and stood there, watching the rubble burn. The last remnants of the steel façade, bent and twisted, brought to mind Roman columns I'd seen earlier in the week. A month or so later

94

I thought about the apocalyptic imagery in *Americans*, found an old copy of the play, and re-read it for the first time in more than a decade. I didn't remember most of the lines. I barely remembered the person who wrote it. But I responded to the underlying intention. Despite the play's faults, it felt more timely than ever. Over the course of the next year I showed the play to family and friends and a few writers whom I respect. The consensus was that I should seek a production. I sent a copy of the play to Dominic Dromgoole, artistic director of the Oxford Stage Company. We'd never met, but I'd read that he liked my first book, *Fast Food Nation*. Dromgoole's enthusiasm for *Americans* is responsible for its present journey from my filing cabinet into the wide world. Nevertheless, I accept full and sole responsibility for every word on the page.

The play's original title was *Fellow Americans*, and its subtitle was "A Tragedy in Two Acts". I decided both were pretentious and got rid of them. I cut a few lines that seemed repetitive or didactic and added a few for the sake of clarity. Otherwise, *Americans* is essentially unchanged. It is what it is. After the passage of so many years, I felt more qualified to edit it than to re-write it. As for the play's historical accuracy, much of the dialogue stems directly from primary sources: speeches, letters, contemporary newspaper accounts. Whenever possible, I let the characters say what they actually said or wrote. *Americans* does contain some deliberate anachronisms and conjectures. For example, Brooks Adams' economic theories did greatly influence Theodore Roosevelt – but Adams' book outlining those theories, *The Law of Civilization and Decay*, was published in 1895. By the time Roosevelt became president, he'd already been persuaded that "the seat of empire" was approaching New York. Moreover, there is no evidence that McKinley's widow and the father of his assassin ever met. Yet there is no proof that they didn't. Throughout the play I tried to remain faithful to the spirit of what really happened. Writing history without footnotes was a real pleasure.

The Leon Czolgosz in *Americans* is largely my creation. Although the biographical details are accurate, historians know little about the man. He shot William McKinley on September 6, 1901 – and was executed only seven weeks later. On the basis of interviews with family members and associates, investigators felt confident that Czolgosz was an anarchist. But few published statements can reliably be attributed to him. "I killed President McKinley because I done my duty," he wrote on September 6, in a brief, handwritten confession. "I didn't believe one man should have so much service [power] and another man should have none." At his trial Czolgosz said, "No one else told me to do it, and no one paid me to do it." At his execution, while strapped to the electric chair, he refused to apologize or seek mercy. "I killed the President because he was the enemy of good people, good working people," he told the spectators. "I'm not sorry for my crime." Czolgosz was so despised that every effort was made to blot him out of history. After the execution, prison authorities burned his clothing and possessions, then poured acid over his corpse, so that no trace of him would remain.

To create the character "Leon Czolgosz", I mixed elements of late-nineteenth-century American anarchists with those of leading anti-imperialists. Although nobody knows if Czolgosz held the views attributed to him in the play, many of his contemporaries certainly did. The conquest of the Philippines provoked an angry national debate about imperialism. William Jennings Bryan, the Democratic candidate for President in 1900, argued that the most important question of the campaign was: "Republic or Empire?" Bryan was soundly defeated by McKinley, but popular distrust of militarism and imperialism endured in the United States for another fifty years. The political beliefs that Czolgosz embraces in the play were not unusual. His violent means of expressing them, however, his "propaganda of the deed", set him apart. As written, Czolgosz shares a number of personal characteristics with other American assassins and terrorists. They tend to be young, white, male, alienated and childless. Their acts can be viewed as political protests or high-minded suicides – or both. Timothy McVeigh, who was convicted and executed for bombing the Oklahoma City federal building in 1995, fit the same profile. Much like Czolgosz's crime, the brutality of McVeigh's bombing received a great deal of attention, while the reasoning behind it got almost none.

The one character who deserves more time on stage – who deserves a play of his own, perhaps, or even a series of plays – is Theodore Roosevelt. In *Americans* he is power and empire incarnate; and Roosevelt was in fact that. But he was also much more than that. He was one of the most extraordinary public figures the United States has produced. Now that I'm forty-four, I have a fuller appreciation of the man. By the time Theodore Roosevelt was my age, he'd already written nearly a dozen books, worked as a cattle rancher, served as the police commissioner of New York City, an undersecretary of the U.S. Navy, a lieutenant colonel in the U.S. Army, Governor of New York State, Vice President of the United States, and President. The assassination of McKinley deepened his concern about the threat of social disorder. As president, Roosevelt became an outspoken opponent of corporate misbehavior and a friend of labor. He not only wrote books, he read them – even books by socialists like Tolstoy and Upton Sinclair. Roosevelt had the courage of his convictions. At the outbreak of the Spanish–American War, he resigned from the Navy Department and joined the army. He was forty years old and had six children. Having lobbied for this war, he was willing to face personal risk in battle. Imagine one of the leading figures in the George W. Bush administration or in Tony Blair's government resigning to fight beside the troops in Iraq. It's hard to imagine, since none of them did. No single work of fiction or non-fiction can capture the true measure of Theodore Roosevelt. I suggest reading the three-volume collection of his letters.

In retrospect, the same fundamental issue was at stake during the presidential elections of 1900 and of 2000: republic or empire? Imperial power has once again become fashionable. In London and Washington, D.C., you hear suggestions that perhaps the British Empire wasn't such a bad idea after all – and that an American empire, properly administered, might do a lot of good. Such arguments have been well received in today's political climate. For some reason, celebrations of the British Empire are not welcomed the same way in India, Pakistan, Kenya or South Africa. The whole notion of selfless conquest, of a "White Man's Burden", was always a lie. Outside of Rudyard Kipling's poem (written in 1899 to persuade Americans to keep the Philippines), the real burden was borne by the colonized, not the colonizer. Although British rule may have conferred some lasting benefits, altruism was hardly the guiding force of that empire – or of any other. "Destiny" can also be ruled out as a plausible explanation, despite the many attempts throughout history to claim it as one. President McKinley described America's acquisition of the Philippines as "a gift from the gods", failing to mention that under-secretary of the Navy Roosevelt (a great man, yes, but not divine) had secretly ordered the American fleet to Manila. As one historian of the phenomenon has observed, "destiny" tends to be invoked in the very circumstances which, upon further analysis, seem to give it least justification.

A century ago those who questioned America's god-given right to rule the world were often accused of treason, an accusation frequently made today. Mark Twain is now considered the quintessential American novelist, yet he too was called a traitor for opposing the annexation of the Philippines. Twain was thought un-American. "*Shall we?*," he asked, attacking McKinley's foreign policy. "Shall we go on conferring our Civilization upon the peoples that sit in darkness, or shall we give those poor things a rest? Shall we bang right ahead in our old-time, loud, pious way, and commit the new century to the game; or shall we sober up and sit down and think it over first?" Twain suggested a new flag for America's imperial conquest: the American flag, with the white stripes painted black, and the stars replaced by a skull and crossbones.

"There are two important things in politics," Mark Hanna once said. "The first is money, and I can't remember the second." During the 1896 presidential campaign that brought McKinley to power, Hanna raised an estimated $16 million for the Republican party. The Democratic candidate, William Jennings Bryan, raised just $425,000. The fundraising skills of Mark Hanna later earned the admiration of Karl Rove, President George W. Bush's chief of staff. Bush's presidential campaign in 2000 was partly inspired by Hanna's 1896 strategy, and Rove has cited McKinley as one of his favorite presidents. It is extraordinary how the events of a hundred years ago still affect our daily lives. And it is chilling to think that decisions being made today will determine the happiness and well-being of millions not yet born, the grandchildren of our children, a hundred years from now. As William Faulkner so eloquently noted, the past is never dead. It isn't even past.

World Premiere, 2003

It's very rarely that the answerphone brings anything but disappointment, so when I returned home to a message from Eric Schlosser, my heart and my imagination leapt a little. I had read and massively admired *Fast Food Nation*. It had woken me up. It was the first in that barrage of books, including those by Naomi Klein and George Monbiot, which blew the sleep out of the eyes of the political sense of a whole generation. It was almost as if a whole consciousness had been blissed to sleep through the blithely complacent nineties. Everyone was long overdue a wake-up call. It took the thoughts and reports of Schlosser and crew, together with the actions and reactions of the oil kids Osama and George, to ring the alarm. The book meant a lot.

However, there was a certain disappointment when I excitedly returned his call and he told me that he'd written a play. Sometimes it seems as if there's hardly been a person I've met throughout my career as a new-play producer – whether Disney executive or philosopher or adventurer or cabinet minister – who hasn't deflated their status and their mystery by waiting for a suitable opening then whispering, "Well, actually, I've written this play. . .". So it was with mixed feelings that I awaited its arrival.

The first feeling on reading it was excitement. This is a big story, and theatre rarely does big stories any more. It has no cheap tricks of suspense or coincidence to pull it together. It just has good old-fashioned Brechtian or Shakespearean sweep. There are a lot of people, these are important events, and the play captures beautifully the mysterious momentum that gives public events a ghastly inevitability. There is a peculiar momentum created by the pressure of history and the hysteria of the media and the weight of public expectation that somehow turns chance into pattern. Eric, as an astute journalist and a historian, has a great nose for that momentum.

The more mature feeling was appreciation of a really fine history play. There have been too few of these recently – the play that uses history as a refracting lens to tell us where we came from and helps us see which way we're going. As with those other loose historians Shakespeare and Brecht, Eric has sufficient disrespect to make art of history, and sufficient respect to see art in history. The play glides between the definite and the invented with a deft and light touch.

And, it's playable. Many plays by writers from other media, especially those that use prose, would drive actors running and screaming from the rehearsal room. But this is speakable, the people are people, the creation of different atmospheres is sure, and the story is economically told. It's not a perfect play, it's a first play. Yet sometimes first plays contain the most electricity.

Then there was the pertinence of the play to appreciate. This is in the realm of the downright weird. Although written in 1985, it discusses an event from 6 September 1901 whose parallels with the events of 11 September 2001 are so chillingly close that I think they will have to be left to the Internet conspiracy theorists to work out. Although this deals with distant and forgotten moments, somehow the play almost now seems too hot to touch. It's extraordinary the process by which stories that are negligible become stories that matter. Eric seems to have latched on to one here.

Then there is what the play says. I don't actually presume to know what this is. All the characters express a certain view, all the views have weight. Each of them has an idea of what America is, and an idea of what it could and should be. All of those ideas matter, which is good play-writing. I know that the play expresses a lot of ideas through speech and action, and I know that that is important now. We need ideas about truth, and democracy, and accountability, and guilt, and innocence, and justice. We need them now, and we need them in public spaces like the theatre. The more the better. The world is full of clouds of confusion and miasmas of chicanery. We need clean, cold, solid sense right now. We are lucky to have Eric's contribution, and we are proud to be doing his play.

Dominic Dromgoole,
Artistic Director, Oxford Stage Company

Americans, first presented at the Arcola Theatre by the Oxford Stage Company, 28 October 2003.